"Full of impactful quotes and anecdotes that will most definitely be shared from my pulpit for years to come, *Peace over Perfection* is written with authentic vulnerability, empathetic understanding, and a deep insight into the heart of God toward his bumbling yet beloved children. Writing as one who has walked and frequently fallen from the arduous tightrope so familiar to fellow perfectionists, Faith invites us off our tightropes altogether, offering us a far better vision that neither downplays our flaws nor cheapens God's love, but locates us within the firm and tender (nail-pierced) hands of God in order that we might experience the true depths of our sin and yet never without the even higher heights of God's grace."

Rev. Andrew Ong, Pastor of Care and Discipleship, Christ Church East Bay, Berkeley, CA

"Faith Chang is a natural storyteller, a gifted writer, and insightful and encouraging. In my anxious pursuit of perfection, Chang points me to Christ—the founder and perfecter of our faith—and his perfect love casts out my fear."

Aaron Lee, Editorial Curator, SOLA Network; Social Media Officer, First Chinese Baptist Church of Walnut, CA

"Reading this book is like sitting down in a comfortable room with your dear friend, both of you tired after a long day. Faith reminds you of how much you are loved and invites you to lean your head on her shoulder while you both take it all in—the weariness of your souls and the grace of your Savior. Accept this invitation to linger on the Lord's love and rest."

Remley Gorsuch, Westminster Kids Manager, Westminster Bookstore; pastor's wife

PEACE OVER

faith chang

enjoying
a good
God when you
feel you're never
good enough

PERFECTION

To Jeff, for being my safe place.

To Mom and Dad, for your love.

Peace over Perfection
© Faith Chang 2024

Published by:
The Good Book Company

thegoodbook.com | thegoodbook.co.uk
thegoodbook.com.au | thegoodbook.co.nz | thegoodbook.co.in

ISBN: 9781784989859 | JOB-007657 | Printed in India

Cover design by Drew McCall

CONTENTS

INTRODUCTION

Return, O my soul, to your rest; for the
Lord has dealt bountifully with you.

PSALM 116:7

As I write these words, my stomach is in knots. I have a vague feeling that I'm being neglectful of unspecified but important responsibilities. I'm afraid I'm getting these sentences wrong. I don't fear that my writing will be inconsequential or ignored as much as I fear that somehow my words *will* be read—and end up doing more harm than good. I distrust my motivations and question whether I'm being self-indulgent, or even sinning in putting these words out into the world.

This isn't merely writer's doubt. This is Christian perfectionism.

The thought comes to mind: *have I spent enough time in devotions today to justify spending time writing about God?* Behind the question is the insinuation that if I haven't read the Bible and prayed enough, I'm being a huge hypocrite right now, just writing empty words. It is an iteration of my deepest fear: that try as I might to obey God, I am actually doing wrong by him and bringing him deep displeasure. I don't hear that accusation as loudly as I used to, but it is still locked and loaded, my heart in its crosshairs.

Perhaps you are familiar with that voice of accusation and self-doubt. It's in the persistent, low-grade fear that you're about to unintentionally slip into sin; the constant discouragement that you're not as joyful, selfless, humble, or loving as you should be as a Christian; the feeling that no matter how hard you try, you'll never serve others, evangelize, or enjoy God enough.

Many Christians, often without realizing it, struggle with a kind of spiritual perfectionism. I've seen it in college students gripped with anxiety about missing God's will and in faithful believers in their sixties who feel as though God is always unhappy with them. I've witnessed it in teens doubting the genuineness of their faith because they struggle with sin and in ministry leaders who are constantly suspicious of their own motives. It can manifest in something as subtle as minor decision-paralysis or intensify to the level of religious OCD. The specifics may vary, but the anxiety, guilt, and weariness are the same.

Theologian D.A. Carson describes this perfectionism:

Occasionally one finds Christians, pastors and theological students among them, who are afflicted with a similar species of discouragement. They are genuinely Christ-centered. They have a great grasp of the gospel and delight to share it. They are disciplined in prayer and service. On excellent theological grounds, they know that perfection awaits final glorification; but on equally excellent theological grounds, they know that every single sin to which a Christian falls prey is without excuse. Precisely because their consciences are sensitive, they are often ashamed by their own failures—the secret resentment that slips in, the unguarded word, the wandering eye, the pride of life, the self-focus that really does preclude loving one's neighbor as oneself. To other believers who watch them, they are among the most intense, disciplined, and holy believers we know; to themselves, they are virulent failures, inconsistent followers, mere Peters who regularly betray their Master and weep bitterly.[1]

You can sincerely believe the gospel and love Jesus while struggling, even to the point of despair, with never feeling good enough before God.

A few years ago, in a small corner of the internet, I wrote an article for believers struggling with this kind of Christian perfectionism. Much of what I'd read and heard addressed to Christians struggling with perpetual fear and guilt in their relationship with God had never really resonated with me. I'd read true biblical words by pastors and counselors about shame, anxiety, and perfectionism, but they never felt like they were *for me*. So I wrote some reflections on what I'd been learning, hoping to offer comfort and hope to other weary strugglers.

The article seemed to strike a chord. People let me know how they were helped—how they had the same anxiety and guilt but hadn't known how to address it. One reader commented, "This put into words something I struggled with, but was even unable to diagnose myself. I just had heard it equated to legalism, but I knew I was not justified by my works. So I was confused [about] what exactly was wrong with me and how to fix it." And another: "I am overwhelmed to hear that there may be rest for my soul, not just in the grace of salvation but in my struggle to love sincerely, to be joyful always, to delight myself in the Lord."

This book was born out of that blog post, except that now, several years later, I write with even more conviction that I'm not the only one who struggles as I do, and that God has much to say to us about this "species of discouragement"—both in his word and through his people in generations past.

The preacher Charles Spurgeon once said, "You will glorify God by resting."[2] He was referring to the words of the psalmist in Psalm 116:7:

> *Return, O my soul, to your rest;*
> *for the LORD has dealt bountifully with you.*

This is the premise of this book: that there is a rest that God gives to Christians which is ours to return to again and again, and it is found in the way he interacts with us. Together, we'll explore how God deals with us as imperfect people and find that he is far more merciful, righteous, loving, and gracious than we may have dared to believe. I have great hope that as we behold him and his ways with us, our souls will find the rest we desperately need.

I write as a student of God's word with a background in Human Development. Where appropriate, I've gleaned important points from psychological research on perfectionism to help broaden our perspective as we consider what God has to say to us in the Scriptures. Between chapters, I've written out some prayers for different situations that Christian perfectionists often face. You can pray these as you finish each chapter or return to them as needed.

As perfectionism is not something we can work through alone, I've included questions for discussing each chapter in a group study or with a friend, as well as resources for further study (p 167). Some readers may also find it beneficial to meet with a mental-health professional if they find themselves needing different specific helps beyond the scope of this book. I've tried to note when this may be the case.

This book is for weary believers who strive to serve God but find themselves weeping bitterly over their failures more often than not. It's for those who have been told they are too hard on themselves but don't know how to pursue holiness without a self-berating inner voice. It's also for those who've become so burnt out by the impossibility of living up to God's standards that they are ready to give up. And it is for those who do not struggle in this way but want to understand and help those who do.

With fear and trembling, I offer these meditations for the weary, anxious, scrupulous, never-good-enough Christian perfectionist. I pray that through these pages, both I (writing now) and you (by God's providence reading) will see how God has dealt bountifully with us, so that our souls can return to their rest and, in resting, bring glory to him.

To the one who seeks to love the Father but has trouble sensing his delight.

To the one who trusts in the gospel of peace but is gripped with anxiety about making mistakes.

For the one whom the Spirit indwells yet who despairs about the slowness of her sanctification.

For the one who is deeply loved beyond his wildest dreams yet rarely feels that way.

These words are for you. These words are for us.

CHAPTER 1

THE PERFECTIONIST'S ACHE

In this fallen world, sadness is an act of sanity,
our tears the testimony of the sane.

ZACK ESWINE

"Tell me a story 'bout God."* My little girl burrows into her
bedsheets, looks up from her pillow, and waits. Taking
her cue, I begin our usual pre-nap liturgy.

Me: "In the beginning God created the…"

Together: "… heavens and the earth."

We speak of each day. The sun, moon, and "twinkle stars"
on day four. Every animal we can think of on day six. It's our
own improvised bit of prose, punctuated with the poetry of
our practiced refrain:

Me: "And God said it was…"

Her: "Good."

Me: "And it was…"

Her: "Good."

To be human is to inhabit God's good earth. For me, it is
to marvel at the generosity of the Creator as I put my toddler
down for a nap. I brush her hair out of her face and nuzzle my
nose into her belly. She laughs, loud and free. Man and woman
were naked and unashamed in the garden (Genesis 2:25).
"Behold," the biblical writer says, "it was very good" (1:31).

My youngest is not yet old enough to understand what comes after our beloved creation story, but her brother is. Watching a video for Sunday school, my little guy twists around in his chair to look away from cartoon Adam and Eve. He is genuinely afraid because he knows the story and anticipates what's coming. "They're going to eat the fruit," he tells me, anxiously. It's not the serpent he's scared of. It's the disobedience.

I don't make him face the screen or say anything to make him feel better about the scene he dreads. That he feels a bit of the horror of the cosmic treason committed by our first parents is not wrong. He will not understand the world in which he's growing up in any other way. He will not understand himself either.

To be human is to inhabit God's good earth, yes—but with the knowledge that it is deeply broken, us included. It is to long for perfection, even as it lies beyond—and behind—us.

PERFECTIONISM'S TOUCH

What is perfectionism? Psychologists who study perfectionism define it as a personality disposition characterized by extremely high standards and overly critical self-evaluations.[3] These two characteristics are known as "perfectionistic strivings" and "perfectionistic concerns."

Perfectionistic strivings—a person's high standards and drive for perfection—can be beneficial in circumstances where focused ambition and high standards of performance foster success. But the problem for perfectionists is that perfectionistic *strivings* are accompanied by perfectionistic *concerns*. These include (but aren't limited to) excessive concern about making mistakes, fear of negative evaluations, self-criticism, and doubts about actions.[4]

Most perfectionists don't experience these strivings and concerns in all areas of life. Rather, their perfectionism is focused on select domains such as sports, work, academics, relationships, physical appearance, or—as is my case, and perhaps yours since you've made your way to this book—spirituality.[5]

Growing up, because I wasn't a perfectionist in stereotypical ways, I didn't think I was one at all. I wasn't stressed about grades or overtly competitive with peers. I have never looked particularly put together, and I share pretty openly about my mistakes. Only in recent years have I come to see the way perfectionism has marked my walk with God for decades.

Here's what perfectionism in my spiritual life—what I'll be referring to as "Christian perfectionism" from here out—looks like for me.

Perfectionism is an anti-Midas, turning my moments dark at the slightest touch. I know it's not fair to expect, say, 19-year-old me to have acted as I would now, but when I think about my past, the predominant feeling is often regret. Especially regarding relationships, I'll wonder why I missed a need, or I'll wish I'd been a different person. *I should have cared more, been more attentive, known better.*

Perfectionism brushes up against the desires I have to do good, and what was once a joyful, exciting opportunity to love others becomes beset with self-doubt and questioning. *Am I doing this for the right reasons? Will I be able to do this well enough? Will this person really be helped? What if I do more harm than good?*

In the past, when I have suffered larger failures and committed bigger sins, I have been plunged into despair. *You will never be good enough. You're useless. You're fake. Are you sure you're a Christian? You don't love. See? You are so self-centered, even now in your supposed repentance.*

Nowadays, my perfectionism tends to be more subtle: a low-level guilt or anxiety lurking in my gut when I'm trying to rest. The feeling at the end of the day that I didn't do all I should have, even when I'm not sure what I neglected.

Perhaps you are familiar with this anxiety and guilt, negative self-talk, rumination over mistakes, or decision-paralysis. These "perfectionistic concerns" crop up in your daily life as a follower of Christ.

Given how distressing our perfectionistic concerns are, it may seem fitting to start this book by saying that the problem lies upstream in our "perfectionistic strivings." That is, the problem is that we *want* to be perfect. And if the problem is our desire for perfection, then the solution to our guilt and anxiety seems simple enough: stop wanting to be perfect.

But is that really it? Are we wrong to want to be perfect? Is the pursuit of perfection a fool's errand—or, even worse, a symptom of people-pleasing, pride, or gospel-less religion, as some might suggest? Or could it be that something more is going on?

As much as it would be simpler to dismiss wholesale our perfectionistic strivings and concerns, the reality is more complicated than that. Our perfectionism hints at larger truths, and before we can find help for it, we need to pay attention to what it's telling us. Rather than silence our desire for perfection, we need to listen to its witness—which is what we'll be doing for the remainder of this chapter.

THE SANITY OF THE PERFECTIONIST'S LAMENT

To be clear, the drive to be perfect can be tied to sinful motives and behaviors. Perfectionism can be rooted in pride and lead us to project a false image of ourselves for human praise. It also can stem from the false belief that our good deeds add to the finished work of Christ on the cross.

But in my experience, most Christian perfectionists buckling under the weight of a tortured conscience, sorrowful over even the smallest of sins, and desperately wanting to do right by God, do not merely want to be *appear* perfect. Nor are they trying to gain entrance into the kingdom of God with works they know are tainted. Rather, they are longing for a perfection commanded by God himself (Matthew 5:48). If this is you, hear this affirmation: *your desire for perfection is not wrong.*

Years ago, I stumbled upon an editorial by theologian D.A. Carson that shed much needed light on the heart of my own perfectionism. In the piece (which I quoted in the introduction), Carson describes genuine, Christ-centered believers who understand and love the gospel yet still struggle with despair over their sin. Up until then, I'd largely heard Christians address perfectionism in terms of pride or unbelief in the gospel. But Carson writes of a "species" of perfectionism that isn't a matter of ego or doctrine. Rather, those who struggle with this type of perfectionism are "so uncomfortable with their wrestlings [over sin] because they know they *ought* to be better."[6]

This is the crux of the Christian perfectionist's struggle. It isn't fundamentally a desire for praise or a lack of faith in the saving work of Christ. It is that we ought to be better—and we know it.

I feel this as a parent: the weight of my careless words, my snap judgments, my deferring of blame because *I'm the mom, and I'm doing so much for you already.* My grief over my failures to be or do as I ought isn't just about my sense of self. I know my sin hurts those around me. Most grievously, it is an affront to the Father whom I am meant to image in my parenting.

Such are my deepest regrets, whether with regards to family, friendships, or ministry. They are bound not primarily to a sense of having failed but in how my failures hurt the ones I claim to love most deeply and how they grieve the God who has only ever been good to me.

We who have tasted the riches of God's mercy to us in Christ, who know the great price he paid to redeem us from our futile ways, know there is no excuse for continued acts of rebellion against our good and gracious King. Thus, it is appropriate to respond to our sin with great grief. "In this fallen world, sadness is an act of sanity, our tears the testimony of the sane," writes one of my favorite authors.[7] Could it be that the Christian perfectionist's lament over imperfection is, in fact, an act of sanity?

I have a good friend who is the kind of Christ-follower I want to be. She is tender-hearted, generous, and compassionate. So when she says she's been convicted by God about being impatient with those around her, I wonder if she's being too hard on herself. Yet something strikes me as holy and sensible in her confessions. She is not trying to be justified before God through good behavior. She is walking in his light, and in her presence, my own rationales for being quick-tempered with my family are exposed as poor excuses. There is something orienting about speaking with a friend who grieves deeply over her sins.

The tears of the Christian perfectionist testify that something is *not* good in this world—that something is broken within us. We were meant to be different, and we know it deep down because this desire to be better—to be perfect—is rooted back in Eden's very good soil.

PERFECTIONISM'S REMEMBRANCE

I didn't realize how much I'd internalized East Coast weather until moving to Los Angeles to do college ministry. Southern California's perpetual sunniness jarred me in the most mundane ways. On campus, club banners gave me pause because they were made of paper, not waterproof vinyl. I handed out flyers for a barbecue and wondered why we hadn't listed a rain date. Fully upholstered couches left out on lawns reminded me I wasn't home. New York, apparently, had trained me to always account for the possibility of precipitation.

We aren't always conscious of it, but our bodies, hearts, and minds have been trained by a post-Edenic world. Without a second thought, we turn back in the parking lot to click our key fobs. We call the doctor's office to schedule annual checkups. We throw on a t-shirt and jeans coming out of the shower, in tacit acceptance that Eden's *naked and unashamed* is not our reality.

Many of us don't think much of it until the *not good* stares us in the face. Groceries in hand, we return to a popped trunk lock. The doctor looks concerned and orders some tests, and we walk away wondering if our lives are about to turn upside-down. We make ourselves vulnerable in a relationship and end up feeling the burn of shame.

The *not good* in the world doesn't just surround us; it is present inside us, and this is where the Christian perfectionist feels it most persistently. All of us, churchgoers or not, know what it's like to wrestle internally as our consciences testify against us (Romans 2:15). Even at four, one of my daughters appealed as she was about to be disciplined, "But everyone sins!" Only the self-deluded or liar would claim otherwise.

Yet, as common as our experience of sin may be, the way we interpret it varies. I remember a high-school math teacher musing that our imperfections make us interesting. Life would be boring if everyone were perfect, she said, and I wondered about the truthfulness of her statement. Would we really not prefer a perfect world? Is life being "interesting" worth the suffering that humans inflict on one another? Those of us who've lived in the wreckage caused by moral failure—our own and others'—know there's nothing endearing about sin.

To be sure, there are times when we need to reject the world's definition of perfection. Our career paths, bodies, homes, and personalities don't have to look like everyone else's in order to be worthwhile and celebrated. Students need room to make mistakes as they tackle calculus. Scientists need to feel free to fail in order to make breakthroughs. But I think my teacher's intent was more than just to reject harmful cultural norms or make space for learning and exploration. It was also an attempt to make sense of the fact that the only world we've known is one full of imperfect people.

Sometimes, sin can feel like such a given that we begin to believe that it is intrinsic to being human. *If no one is perfect*, we reason, *maybe being imperfect is better than being perfect. Maybe the solution to perfectionism is to embrace our sinful imperfections. Maybe perfection is boring.* We forget that being human and erring weren't always inextricably linked: that there were two who, for a time, were pure and undefiled as they walked before God. Humanity then knew the word of their Maker and possessed the power to follow it completely. *And it was very good.*

It is, of course, the holy Scriptures that teach us this. We know that, just like Adam and Eve, we were meant to be perfect. We also know that when they ate from the tree of the knowledge of good and evil, they forfeited life (Genesis 3:16-18). Their disobedience alienated them from God and brought death to all who followed. Our work has become choked by thorns; our consciences, stained with guilt; our natures, corrupted.

The Bible says that because of the sinful nature we've inherited from Adam, apart from an act of God, we are unable and unwilling to choose obedience and life (Romans 5:12-14). We don't do the good we want to do, and we do the evil we know we shouldn't (7:19). In this doing and not doing, we sin against God and destroy one another. We have broken our peace with him, and so we ourselves are broken.

Christians call humanity's rebellion and its consequences "the fall." The power to do good and only good, to be at true peace with one another, to live in righteousness and in communion with God—perfection—this is what we've fallen *from*.[8]

What would it have been like to have our heart, mind, and soul aligned with the will of God at every point? To have been able to give ourselves fully to him in joyful worship at all times? *To be perfect?* It would've been life as it was meant to be.

So it is that our longing for perfection is an ache for what we lost. In that way, it is an ancient ruin of sorts—a remembrance and reminder of the glory of old, of what we once were.

They're going to eat the fruit. And so will all of us in their wake. But it was not always this way. *It was very good.*

PERFECTIONISM'S LONGING

The desire for perfection is in part a mournful look at our Edenic past, but it is not only this. It is also a yearning for a kingdom we would have received as a gift had we not believed it was ours to be grasped. We long for a future that was meant to be ours.

Adam and Eve weren't destined to be in Eden indefinitely as it was. A garden inhabited by a naked couple may seem like an idyllic honeymoon spot, but few of us wish we lived there. That's because the garden was just a seed—the starting point from which the first people were meant to be fruitful and multiply. Our first father and mother were to be rulers: royalty imaging God's reign on earth. Under them, creation would develop into its full potential. Through obedience to God, humanity would inherit an everlasting, cultivated, perfect world.

Though we usually define perfection by what it isn't— "without fault," "flawless" or "free from error"—the fuller meaning of the word is "absolute" or "complete." In the Scriptures, the word carries the sense of something achieving its final purpose.[9] In other words, perfection isn't sterile and boring but rich and full. It isn't the typo-free essay; it's the finished piece moving the reader to tears. It smells more like the sweet nectar of a spring garden than the antiseptic of a surgery room.

We were meant for this kind of perfect world, defined not only by a lack of sin, sickness, and death but by the fullness of human flourishing. Imagine a place where scientific discovery always led to deeper praise and human ingenuity to the good of others. Think of the beauty of fireworks without weapons powered by the same physical processes, or the usefulness of the internet without the dregs of pornography and trolling. Creation would not be exploited but well-tended, and every image-bearer would be treated with the dignity they deserve.

For the individual, a perfect world wouldn't mean uniformity. Far from cookie-cutter sameness, each person would be the truest version of themselves, worshiping God and contributing to society in a way no one else in all of history ever had or ever would. Every morning would start with promise, each day would prove that hope fulfilled, and each night would close with the satisfaction of having done good work before the face of God.

Many of the desires of the Christian perfectionist—to obey God perfectly, to always do what's right for the good of others, to be the best version of ourselves—are in part a vision of the perfect world we were meant for. Herein lies the Christian perfectionist's plight. We carry a sense of Eden and what was promised there, even from the other side of the flaming sword (Genesis 3:24). Barred from the garden, our longings bear witness to what could have been.

AN INVITATION TO MUDDLE

All Christians are meant to desire perfection, but not every Christian struggles with perfectionism. Many are able to grieve over their sin and pursue perfection without an endless undercurrent of guilt, anxiety, and discouragement. So why is it that some faithful believers struggle with Christian perfectionism while so many do not?

Carson poses this question in his article on perfectionism, and though he doesn't give a definitive answer, he offers an observation. The Bible presents us with absolute standards for holiness and faith. These standards would generate despair if not also for the stories of the failures of God's people. The narratives offer us some measure of comfort by showing us that even our heroes in the faith fell short. We need both the Bible's absolute standards *and* the realism of its narratives. Carson writes, "Most of us, I suspect, muddle along with a merely intuitive sense of how these twin biblical heritages ought to shape our lives."[10]

Many Christians are able to intuit their way through life, acknowledging both God's demands for their holiness and their present sinfulness. But while others muddle along, the Christian perfectionist gets stuck.

How can I pursue holiness without constant self-doubt if I know I'm going to sin again? How can I seek to obey God without being paralyzed by fear of falling? How can I have peace and joy in my relationship with God when I keep failing him?

In other words, *how can a Christian perfectionist find rest?*

Jesus once spoke to those exhausted in their pursuit of God:

Come to me, all who labor and are heavy laden, and I will give you rest. Take my yoke upon you, and learn from me, for I am gentle and lowly in heart, and you will find rest for your souls. For my yoke is easy, and my burden is light. (Matthew 11:28-30)

Although this passage is often used to encourage those who are tired in a general sense, Jesus was addressing something more specific and of particular help to us. His 1st-century Jewish listeners would have recognized the language of "yoke" as referring to a confession of monotheism and a commitment of obedience to God's law. This yoke was "taken up" when a person became Jewish and whenever they obeyed the law.[11]

Laboring under the harsh standards imposed by the Jewish religious leaders, Jesus' listeners had grown weary under what they thought were God's demands. The religious teachers of the day had tied up heavy burdens and laid them on their followers without lifting a finger to help (23:4). Knowing this, Jesus says, *Take up* my *commandments,* my *yoke and* my *burden; learn from* me *instead.*

Twice in this short passage Jesus promises rest, harkening back to God's words through the prophet Jeremiah: "Stand by the roads, and look, and ask for the ancient paths, where the good way is; and walk in it, *and find rest for your souls*" (Jeremiah 6:16a). Where is this ancient path? Where is this good way we can walk in without weariness? *It is with me*, says Jesus.

The Christian life is hard. Even with Jesus, we are given a burden to carry. But he is committed to the welfare of our souls as he teaches us to take up his yoke. The rest Jesus promises we'll find is the rest he gives, and we receive it by responding to his invitation. When we feel stuck in the tension between his perfect commands and our present sinfulness, he calls us near. *Come*, he says. *Learn from me.*

It is to this coming and learning that the remainder of this book is dedicated. Aching for perfection and imperfectly shouldering his yoke, we are returning to our soul's rest. Together we seek the God who, east of Eden, deals bountifully with us in the ruins.

A PRAYER FOR REST

God,

I am tired.

You have placed in me a burning desire to
live for you. I want to walk worthy of
the gospel and in step with the Spirit. I
want to love others as Jesus loved me. I
want to be perfect as my heavenly Father
is perfect. But daily I fall short of your
glory in thought, word, and deed.

I remember my past failures
and am filled with regret.
I see my present sinfulness
and am overcome with discouragement.
I imagine my future disobedience
and am overwhelmed with dread.

How can I live a life that pleases
you when I am so sinful?
How can I keep pursuing you when I am
so burdened with fear, guilt, and shame?

O God, my soul cries out for relief. If
there's a better way to walk this road of
faith, please lead me. If there is a way
to lay down this burden without laying
down your perfect standards, please
show me. Gentle and humble Savior,

you call the weak, burnt-out, anxious,
discouraged, and despairing to yourself.

Here I am.

Weary and heavy laden,
   I come to you.

Amen

Scripture references: Philippians 1:27; John 13:34; Matthew 5:48

CHAPTER 2

KNOWLEDGE

I read in a periodical the other day that the
fundamental thing is how we think of God. By God
Himself, it is not! How God thinks of us is not only
more important, but infinitely more important. Indeed,
how we think of Him is of no importance except
in so far as it is related to how He thinks of us.

C.S. LEWIS

For some time, I dreaded becoming a modern-day Leah. This strangely vague yet specific fear began to take root in my late teens. I was sure that my as-yet-unknown future husband would, like Jacob in the Old Testament, wake up in horror one day to find that I wasn't the woman he thought he'd made his vows to.

Leah, we can assume, had been forced to pretend to be the woman Jacob loved (Genesis 29:14-30). I didn't want to pretend, but I'd become convinced that that was just who I was: a pretender. All that seemed good about me was fake, given how messed up I was deep down.

The accusation of hypocrisy grew like a weed in my heart until it cast a grim shadow over my future. I never knew how the matrimonial deception would take place—I only felt certain that it would. My fear was compounded whenever I was pursued romantically. *This guy might like me, but it's because he doesn't know me. If he really knew me...*

I don't remember if I finished that thought. But I do remember the shame.

STARTING WITH THE KNOWLEDGE OF GOD

The invitation to come to Jesus is an invitation to be known. As we begin to think about our perfectionism's causes, symptoms, and remedies, we will inevitably be led into a greater knowledge of ourselves. But this territory can feel, to borrow an image from singer-songwriter John Mayer, like a maze with ever-changing walls.[12] So instead, we will begin with a knowledge more foundational than our own, more ancient, and infinitely more important. Not our knowledge of ourselves, or even our knowledge of God, but God's knowledge of us.

One reason why it's important to start with God's knowledge of us is that Christian perfectionism, like most of the human experience, resists simplistic explanations. For one thing, Christian perfectionism can look different in different people. It can even look different in the same person at different times.

One Christian perfectionist lives with an almost audible critical inner voice; another feels like he's always walking on eggshells. One perfectionist questions all her choices; another is militantly defensive about his. (Both are afraid of being wrong.) We may feel super-motivated in our endless spiritual striving or experience so much despair that we stop trying altogether.

To complicate things, not only do the symptoms of perfectionism vary from person to person, but the roots of it do too. Imagine two students exhibiting perfectionistic tendencies in school. They both neglect their health for classwork, obsess over grades, and compare themselves with their peers. The first student is the only one in her immigrant family to make it past primary school. She studies to secure her family's financial future, and the knowledge of this responsibility weighs heavily on her shoulders as she writes papers, making her head throb when she sits for exams. A second student has highly educated parents. He is expected to match or even surpass them in his achievements, just as his sister did. But he's not her. So his dad yells and shames him. He's stupid and worthless, and will never amount to anything. Why? Because he didn't bring home that 4.0. Both students look similar from the outside, but with different motivations behind their perfectionism, they require different help.

This is just as true when it comes to Christian perfectionism. Personality, family history, trauma, spiritual formation, church experience, and cultural backgrounds all contribute to our understanding of God's expectations of us and our responses when we fail to meet them. "The fall brought disruption at *all* levels of our personhood," explains biblical counselor Mike Emlet.[13] Emlet identifies four different areas in which the fall contributes to "scrupulosity" (which is what Christians have historically called a person's intense struggle with Christian perfectionism). These areas are 1) distorted views of God, self, Scripture, and the Christian life; 2) brain-based dysfunction; 3) relational influences; and 4) societal-cultural and situational influences.[14] All of these factors can play into our struggles in complicated ways.

In this sense, perfectionism is more of a syndrome than a disease. Medically, a syndrome is a set of symptoms that commonly occur together but whose exact causes and cures remain unknown. Syndromes recur often enough to warrant a name (for example, "chronic fatigue" or "Kawasaki"), but their underlying causes can be variable or due to a combination of factors.

But if there is no standardized course of treatment for perfectionism and its causes are so complex, how can we be healed? How do we find rest when we're not 100% sure why we're running ourselves ragged in the first place? One of the frustrating things about Christian perfectionism is not always knowing what "our problem" is. We have the sense that something needs to change. We just don't know what that *something* is.

Thankfully, though the causes and fruit of your perfectionism may not be completely identical to anyone else's, there is one by whom the hidden places of your heart are always discerned. Darkness is as light to him, and the parts of you that are obscured even to yourself lie open before him. To him, the tangle of emotions, physiology, motives, experiences, and desires contributing to our perfectionism are plain.

The psalmist in Psalm 139 taught God's people to sing in praise to the one who knows:

> *O LORD, you have searched me and known me!*
> *You know when I sit down and when I rise up;*
>   *you discern my thoughts from afar.*
> *You search out my path and my lying down*
>   *and are acquainted with all my ways.*
> *Even before a word is on my tongue,*
>   *behold, O LORD, you know it altogether.*
>
> (Psalm 139:1-4)

God, who formed you in your mother's womb, knows your temperament, strengths, and weaknesses. He knows what you seek through your attentiveness to your performance and what you want to avoid when you feel tired of trying. He knows the life experiences that have formed you and the way you have interpreted and internalized them. He knows why you fear making mistakes and why you respond in the way you do to failure. And he cares deeply about all of it.

When our perfectionism feels like a labyrinth, we can take heart, knowing we are completely known by God. We may not be able to pinpoint the *something* that needs to change, but that's ok. The success of a heart surgery is dependent on the doctor's knowledge and skill, not the patient's ability to read his own cardiac angiogram. As you take steps to find help for your perfectionism, you don't carry the weight of your own deliverance. Whether you're reading this book, sharing with a friend about your struggle, or receiving counsel and medication from a mental-health professional, you walk the road to rest dependent on your Maker's knowledge of you— and what he chooses to do with this knowledge.

GOD KNOWS YOUR BURDEN

Well-intentioned people often add to the burden of the perfectionist by adding perfectionism to the list of sins he is already plagued with guilt over. I once texted my sister a screenshot of a Christian article meant for perfectionists that I'd found unhelpful. "Ah, the ol' 'tell the perfectionist to try harder' trick," she replied. She's not wrong.

My stomach tightens as I think about all I'm told to do (and not do) in my struggle against perfectionism. *Focus on loving others instead. Believe the gospel more. Be humbler. Submit to God. Repent of your perfectionism. Just stop trying so hard.*

There may be some truth there. Still, these proposed solutions often effectively add to my running list of things

I need to change about myself. In order to *truly* be perfect, I need to stop being a perfectionist—a statement that feels as helpful as someone telling me I ought to be sleeping as I toss and turn in bed. Thankfully, our Savior takes a different approach as we—failing him and eaten up inside because of it—do our best to follow him. He does not berate us for being weary or shame us for our guilt. He sees us lying there, struggling to sleep and dead tired. Thus, his invitation goes out: "Come to me." Why? Because he *knows* we labor and are heavy laden—that we need his rest.

We're starting with Jesus' knowledge of our need because for the perfectionist, the search for rest itself can become plagued with shame, guilt, and anxiety. There can be a sense that if only we trusted God more, believed the right things, changed our patterns of thought, stopped giving way to fear, and had more realistic expectations of ourselves, *then* we wouldn't struggle as we do. Our self-directed accusations boomerang back to us on loop—we feel anxious and tired, then guilty for being anxious and tired, then guilty for feeling guilty, and so on.

So, God steps in.

One of my favorite sentences in the Old Testament is in Exodus. The opening scenes of the book describe the Israelites' bitter oppression under Pharaoh. The people cry out to God for rescue. God hears their groaning and remembers his promises to their forefathers. Then, the writer simply states, "God saw the people of Israel—and God knew" (Exodus 2:25).

"God knew." In the Scriptures, to say that God knew your suffering was to say that deliverance was coming. "I will rejoice and be glad in your steadfast love," the psalmist wrote, "*because you have seen* my affliction; *you have known* the distress of my soul, and you have not delivered me into the hand of the enemy" (Psalm 31:7-8). The psalmist rejoices in being known because God's seeing and knowing is accompanied by his help.

The statement that "God knew" in Exodus is a momentary flinging back of the narrative curtain, a clue to those watching the drama unfold that things are about to change. God sees, God knows, and the stage is set for the incredible rescue to come.

Just as God knew the burdens his people were forced to carry under Pharaoh in the Old Testament, and under religious teachers in the New Testament, God knows your fear, guilt, and shame. And rather than ignore or condemn you for your neediness, this knowledge of your need prompts his loving initiative. He sees your burdens, and he is working to free you from them.

HE KNOWS YOUR IMPERFECTIONS

In a way, God's knowledge of us is a counterintuitive truth to put before perfectionists. It can be comforting to know that he understands our needs—but that the perfect one knows all our secret sins, hidden motives, careless words, and outright disobediences? We tremble at the thought. If we who are unholy are undone by seeing our own sinfulness, how much more must he be offended by our impurities?

In one sense, reverent fear is appropriate in the presence of the holy God. Yet there are also ways in which understanding God's full knowledge of our sins can actually help our hearts rest easier as we walk the path of holy reverence.

For one thing, God's complete knowledge of us assures us that his forgiveness is complete—that when he says he has "forgiven us all our trespasses," he really means every single one (Colossians 2:13). The mistakes that continue to haunt us, the sins we wish we didn't have to confess, the vices we fear giving way to later—he has not failed to note any of it. So we can know that when he declares that *all* our trespasses have been forgiven, truly they are.

God's full knowledge of our imperfections grants us assurance in another way. I have often carried the sense of being a fraud. My perfectionism means the affirmation I receive from others tastes sweet for a moment, only to quickly turn into bitter accusation. *They just don't really know how messed up I truly am.*

I hate the prospect of being thought of more highly than I ought to be, to have hypocrisy added to the list of sins I've committed. The praise of others seems both an indictment and a setup for letting people down. So it is a freeing thought that my relationship with God is not founded upon any misperception on his part.

Years ago, back when the fear of hypocrisy had so filled me that I feared the prospect of a romantic relationship, there was one young man with whom I was uncharacteristically myself. We'd met in college and then worked together in perpetually fair-weathered LA. Without realizing it, I felt free to be more direct and honest with him than with other people. "I can't believe you did that," I once said to him before walking away angry. "She definitely doesn't like me," he'd thought after my rare moment of transparency. I would, though, come to like, love, and marry this man who'd see me in many more unguarded moments. Being loved by him as his wife has been one of the greatest means of God's grace in my life; because, though I felt like Leah, he knew and chose me nonetheless.

It is profoundly healing to have a close friend, parent, sibling, or spouse who has seen us at our worst and is still committed to loving us. These relationships are so often God's means of healing because they are a taste of his love. "To be loved but not known is comforting but superficial," writes the late pastor Timothy Keller. "To be known and not loved is our greatest fear. But to be fully known and truly loved is, well, a lot like being loved by God."[15]

Can anyone know us more completely than God does? Every word spoken and every thought unsaid, every praise- or wrath-worthy act committed was known by God before our birth. People talk about needing to walk into marriage with both eyes open, but we have always been naked before the Lord, who has chosen us and loves us with no false illusions of our goodness. You were fully known to God before you ever thought to call on him. Therefore, nothing about his interactions with you—his forgiveness, his pleasure, his love— is superficial. Because his knowledge of you is complete, you can trust the depths of his love for you.

Theologian J.I. Packer writes of this knowledge:

> *There is tremendous relief in knowing that [God's] love to me is utterly realistic, based at every point on prior knowledge of the worst about me, so that no discovery can now disillusion Him about me, in the way that I am so often disillusioned about myself, and quench His determination to bless me.*[16]

Some of us walk around with a sense that God is perpetually disappointed with us. It feels like he's constantly giving us second chances, hoping that *this time* we'll do better, and we can't bear the thought of how his face will fall the next time we inevitably fail.

God's knowledge of us rewrites the scenes of exposure that we dread; because, though our sins grieve God, he is never *disappointed* in us as if he's only discovered who we *really* are after calling us to follow him. His expectations of us are "utterly realistic, based at every point on prior knowledge of the worst." And while our failures and sins may upend our perception of ourselves, they never take him by surprise. There is tremendous *relief* in this, Packer says. This is the language of rest.

I think of Peter in the Gospels. Like him, I had once been confident in my commitment to my Master. Only after the rooster's crow did we both weep, feeling the fickleness of our hearts—the foolishness of our self-assured declarations that we would follow Jesus to the end. Yet, while Peter's love was untrustworthy, Jesus' love for him was not. He had seen Peter's denial coming from the beginning—had even spoken of it. But he had also told Peter of his hope for him beyond his betrayal (Luke 22:32). Peter was chosen, called, and loved with all his faults in full view.

Beloved, none of God's people have ever pulled a fast one on him, and neither have you. He knows you completely, and nothing you do or don't do will lead to any disillusionment on his part. When you stumble, you may fearfully search his face for a change of his resolve to love you—but you will never find even the slightest flicker in his affections. He is fully committed to the real, whole you. Fully known, you are truly loved.

TO BE KNOWN IS TO BE HIS

I have a childhood memory of visiting my uncle's 100-acre farm in Mississippi. It's fuzzy enough for me to question whether it really happened, but I remember it this way.

During one of our days on his property, my uncle walks my mom and I out to a pasture. It's empty, we're told, because the animals are in the woods. Then—and this is the part I don't expect—my uncle calls out. Within minutes, horses break through a line of trees bordering the field where we wait, and before I know it, they are standing before us. I remember watching my uncle make his rounds to see each horse. I remember most of all my wonder that they returned at his call.

In the Gospel of John, Jesus describes another keeper of animals. Shepherds, he says, call their sheep, and the sheep know the timbre of their master's voice. In the same way, Jesus says, "My sheep hear my voice, and I know them, and they follow me" (John 10:27).

Implied in Jesus' illustration is a different kind of knowing than what we've touched upon thus far. Here is more than the simple knowledge acquired by perception. It is what C.S. Lewis referred to as the infinitely important question of "how God thinks of us." Those Jesus knows are "called in, welcomed, received, acknowledged."[17] God's knowledge of us "implies personal affection, redeeming action, covenant faithfulness and providential watchfulness" explains Packer.[18]

Jesus describes this knowledge in the strongest of terms: "I know my own and my own know me, just as the Father knows me and I know the Father" (v 14-15). As the Father and Son are united in an everlasting and perfect love, the good Shepherd's knowledge of his sheep is strong and steady, relational and intimate, personal and tender. To be known by God is to be in relationship with him.

For the Christian perfectionist, God's loving call of us to himself can often end up being overshadowed emotionally by the call to follow his commands. We begin to relate to him, at least in our day-to-day attitudes and attempts at obedience, primarily as the rule-giver.[19] So we rule-keepers need reminders of the shepherd heart of Jesus. To heed the call of Christ is to hear the voice of one who loves us as we follow him in living, breathing relationship.

Years ago, I watched a segment on muster pilots: Australian cattlemen in the outback who round cattle from the air. In a helicopter, they made sudden descents and turns, hovering dangerously close to the ground to face off stubborn cows. They flushed out small groups of cattle from among the trees until the gathered "mob" numbered 2,000. The animals were then driven for 30 miles by helicopters, horses, and all-terrain vehicles. It was incredible to see the pilots' knowledge and skill as they tapped into the cows' herding instinct. Still, it was quite a different scene than that of my uncle calling to his horses, or a shepherd calling each sheep by name. The cows didn't know who was driving them; they just ran.

I wonder if rather than experiencing the Christian life as sheep following the Shepherd, many of us live as if we are cows flanked by helicopters. Perhaps you have been going for miles and miles, running scared. But your Savior is not a muster pilot; he is the Shepherd.

He doesn't drive you from behind with impersonal commands but calls you by name, guiding you as one who knows you (v 3).

He graciously speaks to you and assures you that you will know his voice (v 16). You don't need to be constantly afraid that you'll miss the way or that you already have.

He laid down his life for you and holds on to you so that you can't be snatched out of his hand (v 11, 28). Not even your own doubt, slow growth, or daily failures can separate you from his grace and mercy.

In love, God invites us to know him as he knows us. Through how he treats us, we are reminded that he is not just the law-giver, but our Friend, Father, and Shepherd. And as we consider how he deals *bountifully* with us, our souls return to their rest (Psalm 116:7).

God is not a harsh overseer, watching over the progress of his people with a whip in hand. This was the slavery the people of Israel cried out to God for deliverance from. Of Pharaoh who set himself up as lord according to the way of the world, demanding the multitudes to "get back to your burdens" (Exodus 5:4). The earth's rulers "lord it over [people], and their great ones exercise authority over them," but not so the Son of Man, who came to serve and give his life as a ransom for many (Matthew 20:25-28).

Our good Shepherd laid down his life for his sheep, and to be known by him is to be his.

SPEAKING OUR NEED TO THE ONE WHO KNOWS

These days, perfectionism for me sounds less like fully formed accusations and more like the eerie film score behind a suspenseful movie scene. I'm not struggling with loud voices of condemnation like I used to, but the knots in my stomach, the reticence to bring my whole self before God—these linger. The soundtrack begins to play, and I tell myself that it's bearable. Or that I know the truth already and should be able to reason my way out of this on my own. God's ways differ from mine, though.

I think of the blind beggar, Bartimaeus, crying out to Jesus from the side of the road. When others finally told him, "Take heart. Get up; he is calling you," Jesus asked him a question that halts me in my tracks. "What do you want me to do for you?" (Mark 10:46-52).

Jesus, who knows all things, asks a man who is blind what he wants him to do for him. Why would he do this?

Perhaps it's because he doesn't just want to make the man better. He seeks the man himself.

Jesus could have healed Bartimaeus from a distance, but instead he stops. He summons this precious image-bearer to himself. And while others had told Bartimaeus to be silent, face to face with Jesus, he is invited to speak. When Bartimaeus is healed, Jesus' face will be among the first—if not *the* first—he sees. And seeing Jesus, he follows him (v 52).

Such is the way of our Lord, not only to know our need but to invite us to name it in his presence. He has taken note of our weariness, imperfections, and sins, and he draws us near that we may be restored to him. He bids us come, that we may know the heart and power of the one who knows us.

What do you want me to do for you? Perfectionist, take heart. Your Shepherd is calling.

A PRAYER FOR WHEN
YOU FEAR YOU'RE A FAKE

God of all, who knows all,

I feel like a fraud. My sins are so great
that I'm not sure my pursuit of you is
genuine. I'm afraid that others think
more highly of me than I deserve.
I dread the next revelation of my
hidden faults and willful sins.

According to your great compassion,
look upon me!
Rescue me, O God who sees me.

Father, though I fear what lies in the
depths of me, you've already seen it
all. You love me with full knowledge
of all I've ever done and will do, who
I've been and who I will be. Remind
me that because I am fully known, I
am and will always be truly loved.

Jesus, I rejoice in your finished work upon
the cross. Thank you that there is no
stain your blood cannot cleanse, not
even the sin of hypocrisy. Let me rest in
your perfect knowledge, which assures
me that your forgiveness is complete.

Holy Spirit, you who test the hearts of all
and know me better than I know myself:

Search me and know my heart,
Test me and know my anxious thoughts,
See if there's any offensive way in me,
And lead me in your everlasting way.

Do this all for your name's sake, O Lord.

In Jesus' name,
Amen

Scripture references: 1 John 1:7; Psalm 139:23-24 (NIV)

CHAPTER 3

MERCY

"Lord, why is this?" I trembling cried.
"Wilt thou pursue thy worm to death?"
"'Tis in this way," the Lord replied,
"I answer prayer for grace and faith."

JOHN NEWTON

It's my sophomore year of college, and the Gothic-style chapel at the center of campus has become a personal sanctuary. Between lectures, I make my way under dim-lit chandeliers to the same dark wooden pew, open my green, compact Bible on the seat, settle cross-legged on the floor, and pour out my heart.

I'd grown up in church, but a new desperation had begun to burn in me at the end of high school. I wanted to know God's will for my life. *My will for you is to love me and know me,* came the reply.

So I begin to search the Scriptures for his voice, praying like he really hears. I'm so certain that God is near and that he will speak to me that sometimes my pace quickens in anticipation as I approach the chapel doors.

Yet seeking God more earnestly than ever, I begin to feel as if a spotlight is fixed on me, revealing sin. Lust and pride, a tongue quick to bring others down, subtle attention-stealing, outright glory-hoarding. The penetrating beam is inescapable. To have it rest on me for a moment would be sobering. But more than a year of relentless unveiling and I am drowning.

It's in this condition that I find myself kneeling between chapel pews, pleading with God again for deliverance from sin and the power it has over me. But on this day, I happen to glance up and notice a painting on the vaulted ceiling above me. A hand points down at an open book. Jesus' words are written across the pages:

*BLESSED ARE THEY THAT
HUNGER AND THIRST AFTER
RIGHTEOUSNESS FOR THEY
SHALL BE FILLED*

I think of the other beatitudes, recalling those of whom Jesus said, "Blessed are..." (Matthew 5:3-12). I'm not pure or persecuted. I'm not meek. But *this* blessing—it only requires desire: hunger and thirst. I know the promise is for me and, believing, lay claim to it in hope.

That God would promise to satisfy my hunger and thirst is a mercy. That he would make me hunger and thirst in the first place—this is mercy too.

THESE INWARD TRIALS

In many ways, the desire for perfection might be called a longing for righteousness. Christian perfectionists want to be righteous—to live in a way that pleases God and to hear him declare his pleasure over our days. This is a good and God-given desire. Sometimes though, perfectionism means we've followed our hunger and thirst for righteousness down a road that's led to a dark place.

Perhaps you're there now. Heart burning, you asked for greater love for God and to be made more like his Son. You've read his word and taken steps of obedience. But decisive victory and transformation haven't come. Instead, you feel *more* guilty and even less like Christ than when you began. Or maybe you feel spiritually dry, like God is far from you and you don't know why. You fear that God is silent because of something you're doing or not doing, though you're not sure what you've done or failed to do.

Am I even a Christian? Am I cursed? What's wrong with me?

Here, it can be helpful just to know that we aren't alone in our troubling thoughts. Years ago, in the throes of deep discouragement, I found this assurance in a poem written by a minister in the 18th century. It resonated with me, and I ended up rereading it so many times that I memorized it without meaning to. The story it tells may feel familiar to you too.

John Newton's "These Inward Trials" begins:

I asked the Lord that I might grow
In faith, and love, and every grace;
Might more of His salvation know,
And seek, more earnestly, His face.

'Twas He who taught me thus to pray,
And He, I trust, has answered prayer!
But it has been in such a way
As almost drove me to despair.

Newton goes on to describe how he hoped God would answer immediately, and "by His love's constraining pow'r, / Subdue my sins, and give me rest." Instead, God makes Newton feel his hidden sins and lets satanic forces assault his soul. It all becomes so unbearable that he asks whether God is trying to kill him.

Throughout history, well-known Christians have recounted such experiences in their pursuit of God. Besides Newton, who famously penned the hymn "Amazing Grace," there is Martin Luther, John Bunyan, and Thérèse of Lisieux.[20] Even the apostle Paul, speaking of the raging battle between his sinful desires and his desire to obey God, wrote, "Wretched man that I am! Who will deliver me from this body of death?" (Romans 7:24).

Knowing that others have walked through similar trials, the question we might consider is: *why?* Why does God so often answer prayers to "subdue [our] sins and give [us] rest" in a way that just about drives us to despair?

IN MERCY, HE WOUNDS

The Puritan theologian Richard Sibbes addresses this question in *The Bruised Reed*, a book that has comforted Christian perfectionists since the 1630s. Borrowing from a metaphor in Isaiah (42:3), Sibbes refers to believers under persistent conviction of sin as "bruised reeds." Encouraging these downhearted Christians, he writes, "Let this support us when we feel ourselves bruised. Christ's way is first to wound, then to heal. No sound, whole soul shall ever enter into heaven."[21]

Before we continue, I want to make it clear what we don't mean here. The "bruising" Sibbes writes of isn't a mind trick or guilt trip. God does not manipulate us psychologically as some evil, abusive people do.[22] There are leaders, even in the church, who push hard into places of shame. They purposely make their listeners feel useless and worthless before proclaiming, "But God loves you!" as if that would lead to profound gratitude rather than whiplashed confusion. *So God thinks I'm despicable, but he loves me?*

God does not work that way, indebting us to himself by stirring up feelings of worthlessness and self-hate. Rather, throughout the Scriptures, he repeatedly affirms our value. Each one of us is wonderfully made by our Creator and we are of great worth to him (Psalm 139:14; Matthew 6:26). Even as sinners, we have dignity because we bear his image (James 3:9). Though he may have hard words for us at times, nowhere in Scripture does he speak about us with contempt. He never casually puts us down just to put us in our place.

God is "too loving to say anything needlessly severe; too true to say anything untrue."[23] Thus in his wounding, he is the faithful friend spoken of in Proverbs, who lovingly speaks words you really need to hear, even—and especially— when you don't want to hear them (Proverbs 27:6a). Our temptation in the shadow of the fall is to deny our sinfulness or try to fix it on our own. Knowing both options are deadly, God makes us confront the painful reality of our situation.

His is the work of the surgeon who cuts in order to expose and remove diseased tissue. God afflicts his people but only as much as necessary for healing and restoration. His wounding causes pain but not harm. It is the mercy described in Hosea, where the prophet, calling God's people to repentance, says, "He has torn us, *that he may heal us*; he has struck us down, *and he will bind us up*" (Hosea 6:1b).

Sin blinds us to itself, so it is in mercy that God brings us to our senses, as disorienting as that may be. For those who haven't known such conviction before, it can feel like freefalling. It is one thing to acknowledge you are imperfect but another to wake up to your utter inability to cleanse or save yourself.

The fall is no mere abstract theological principle. It is right here, in me and ever before me—that twisting and corrupting nature of sin. I have fallen devastatingly short of God's glory. But the good news is that the Judge of heaven and earth is also the great Physician. He did not come for the healthy but for the sick. He did not come for the righteous but for sinners (Luke 5:31). So, in love and with precision, he wounds.

HAVE MERCY ON ME

"God, be merciful to me, a sinner!" Only one who has been wounded by God is able to pray this way. And, as Jesus taught, only one who prays this way can be made righteous. Jesus tells us this through a parable that begins, "Two men went up into the temple to pray" (Luke 18:10).

One of the praying men is a Pharisee. The Pharisee thanks God that he is unlike "other men." He has not stolen, been unjust, or committed adultery. He fasts and gives offerings. He—thank God—is not like "this tax collector" (v 11-12).

"This tax collector" is the other man. He stands far off. He won't even lift his eyes to heaven. He beats his chest in sorrow and prays, "God, be merciful to me, a sinner!" (v 13).

This sinner, says Jesus, *and not the Pharisee, left the temple and went home justified.*

What does it mean that the tax collector went home "justified"? And what does this have to do with the Christian perfectionist's desire for righteousness?

To understand how this story is relevant to us, we begin with why Jesus told it. The Gospel writer says that Jesus' parable was meant for those who "trusted in themselves that they were righteous" (v 9).

In the Scriptures, a righteous person is someone who keeps God's holy standard. The word "righteous" can also carry the idea of being accepted by God. Jesus' teaching was meant for those who believed they were approved of by God because they kept God's laws. Thus, the prayer of the Pharisee.

Now, if the Pharisee had fully obeyed God's laws, he would have had every right to be confident in his righteousness. In fact, he could have legitimately claimed life and blessing based on his adherence to the law. This was the possibility laid out to us in Eden—right standing before God, blessing, and eternal life through obedience. But as a ruler might declare war for a nation, Adam rebelled on behalf of all humanity. So the Pharisee stood guilty on two counts: first, by virtue of being a descendant of Adam; second, because he sinned (most notably, he harbored pride and contempt). Thus, though he believed the law heralded him as righteous, it actually condemned him to death (Romans 7:10).

The tax collector, on the other hand, knew there was no way he could stand before God on his own merit. Knowing divine law condemned him as sinner, he sought mercy instead. And in humbly throwing himself upon the mercy of God, he was justified.

When God justifies someone, he declares as Judge that a person has been fully obedient to the law. The wonder of this story—and the gospel—is that God justifies *sinners*. He proclaims that despite their unrighteous deeds, sinners can be treated as though they have been righteous in the court of divine law.

God is holy, so he doesn't justify sinners by shirking his law and waving off sin. Scripture is clear that the wages of sin is death (6:23), and God does not bend his own rules here. Rather, he maintains his righteousness and shows mercy at great cost to himself. He justifies sinners through his Son, who became sin on our behalf "so that in him we might become the righteousness of God" (2 Corinthians 5:21).

When he walked this earth, Jesus' perfect obedience to the Father meant he deserved divine favor and eternal blessing. But at the cross, he received wrath instead, paying the penalty of our sin. Now, by faith, we are granted the righteous standing he earned through his obedience. Theologians refer to this as the "wonderful exchange"—our sins transferred to Christ, his righteousness to us.

For the Christian afflicted by guilt, the Heidelberg Catechism—a kind of Q&A on the Christian faith used in churches since the 16th century—weaves together beautifully the implications of this wonderful exchange:

> *Even though my conscience accuses me of having grievously*
> *sinned against all God's commandments, of never having*
> *kept any of them, and of still being inclined toward all*
> *evil, nevertheless, without any merit of my own, out*
> *of sheer grace, God grants and credits to me the perfect*
> *satisfaction, righteousness, and holiness of Christ, as if I*
> *had never sinned nor been a sinner, and as if I had been*
> *as perfectly obedient as Christ was obedient for me.*
> *All I need to do is accept this gift with a believing heart.*[24]

The consciences of Christian perfectionists often accuse us of "having grievously sinned" and "still being inclined toward all evil." You may desire to stand righteous before God but feel keenly the ways in which you've failed to live up to his standards. Rather than being left to shrink back from God in these moments or urged to work harder to ease your guilt, you are invited to believe.

By faith, you have received the righteousness of Christ "out of sheer grace." You are counted obedient because of Christ's obedience on your behalf. And though you may feel too sinful to lift your eyes to heaven, unable to manage more than a plea for mercy, that is all that's required of you to be made clean. All you need to do is receive his gift with a believing heart, and you will return home justified.

MERCIFUL RESTRAINT

Only those who know their need for mercy will know the gospel as good news. Therefore, Sibbes writes, before conversion, the painful revelation of our sinfulness "makes us set a high price upon Christ," so that "the gospel becomes the gospel indeed."[25] As in my experience, this sometimes happens after conversion as well. God opens our eyes in new ways to our sinfulness so that we may know more deeply—an experiential, down-to-our-bones kind of knowing—the great grace of having been declared forgiven and righteous in Christ.

But how do we interpret the discouragement over our sin that we continue to feel even as we gladly trust in Jesus' righteousness? How do we make sense of the fact that years, even decades, after we've first started walking with God, we continue to feel this wounding?

One reason why discouragement and guilt can linger even after we've come to know the gospel is because though we have been justified, God is still making us righteous. Describing this dynamic, the Reformer Martin Luther called the Christian *simul justus et peccator*: "at the same time righteous and sinner." Our standing before God is secure, but conversion is just the start of our sanctification (the process of being made holy). Until we see Jesus face to face, we will only experience this perfecting work of God bit by bit in measures—incredible, life-changing, miraculous measures, but measures nonetheless.

When we are born again as children of God, he gives us new hearts, sensitive to his Spirit and his word. We grow in our love for the things he loves, and we begin to hate the evil we used to love. We see the way sin isn't intrinsic to who we were designed to be and how it draws us away from our loving God and our God-given purpose; and we lament its presence in our lives. Sibbes explains that in our sanctification, this sorrow over sin is necessary "that we may reform that which is amiss, though it be to the cutting off of our right hand, or pulling out of our right eye" (a reference to Jesus' words in Matthew 5:29-30).[26] Grief over sin is necessary because it propels us to take radical steps of repentance and obedience.

Long seasons of repentance guided by the Holy Spirit's conviction also grow in us a distaste for sin—the way nausea warns our body away from foods that have made us sick before. In this way, sometimes our wounding is actually God's merciful restraint. The lingering regret, sadness, and pain I carry from my past failures to love and obey God remind me that the sins I used to be enslaved to are just as dangerous to me now. "Before I was afflicted I went astray," wrote the psalmist, "but now I keep your word" (Psalm 119:67). I have learned to be thankful for the limp that keeps me from so easily running back to the things that once brought me death.

At the end of "These Inward Trials," Newton touches upon the sanctifying purposes of God behind these hard seasons. Newton has come to the end of himself, perplexed that God would allow and cause his pain. He writes:

> *"Lord, why is this?" I trembling cried.*
> *"Wilt thou pursue thy worm to death?"*

"'Tis in this way," the Lord replied,
"I answer prayer for grace and faith.

"These inward trials I employ,
From self and pride, to set thee free;
And break thy schemes of earthly joy
That thou may'st find thy all in Me."

Under the tutelage of inward trials, God sets us free from self and pride and pursuit of fleeting joys. He grows in us grace, faith, and dependence on him. And he does all this that we may find everything we truly need in him. Newton's inward afflictions were not evidences of God's disfavor or damnation but proof of holy work being done in his heart. Though he hadn't felt it at first, God was answering his prayer for growth and greater knowledge of himself the whole time.

LIVING BY MERCY

Even as God teaches us to seek his righteousness, he recognizes that he is commanding us to pursue something we cannot attain on our own. "Blessed are those who *hunger and thirst* for righteousness," Jesus says, not because they will claim it by their own grit and determination but because it will come through a promise: *they will be filled.*

Jesus' promise calls to mind an Old Testament image. Speaking to the Israelites on the cusp of entering the promised land, Moses explained that God had let them hunger in the wilderness and fed them manna—miraculous bread from heaven—to teach them "that man does not live by bread alone, but man lives by every word that comes from the mouth of the LORD" (Deuteronomy 8:3). In the same way, God makes us hunger and thirst for righteousness that we may rely on his supernatural provision not only in our justification but in our sanctification as well.

Sometimes, Sibbes writes, we continue to experience heavy conviction of sin after conversion, "to let us see that we live by mercy."[27] This is what God was doing for me in that old university chapel. Up until then, I'd understood my own spirituality as a sort of assignment. I didn't think I could earn heaven through good works, but I pictured the life of Christian obedience as a solo mission fueled by gratitude for Jesus' sacrifice; God had cleansed me of my sin and then sent me off with instructions to live for him.

I needed to learn that although sanctification requires my effort in a way that justification doesn't, I am just as dependent upon God for it. It is the Spirit who transforms me from glory to glory (2 Corinthians 3:18). It is God who works in me to will and work for his good pleasure (Philippians 2:13). He is the one who will sanctify me completely one day (1 Thessalonians 5:23). He will complete the good work he began (Philippians 1:6).

Through a season of wounding, God was indelibly impressing on my heart that the righteousness I sought would only be found in his active work in me. He was slowly teaching me that the Christian life would be by faith and grace to the very end—that there was mercy and power in Christ not just for my pardon but for my lifelong sojourn of being perfected.

THE ACCUSER

In his wounding, God is the most faithful of friends, and though these seasons of inward trials can be distressing, we can trust his heart. With love and patience, he leads us to rest in his work for and in us. But not every voice that wounds is

God's. As we learn to rest in Christ's righteousness, we need to be aware that we have an enemy hell-bent on keeping us from that rest.

Satan's name means "adversary," or "accuser," and in seasons of inward trials, it can be difficult to distinguish between his accusations and the voice of God. In Revelation, he is called the "accuser of our brothers ... who accuses them day and night before our God" (Revelation 12:10). Most of us won't find it hard to imagine the kind of evidence he might bring against us in the heavenly courtroom.

A vision in Zechariah unveils a bit of the nature of these unseen realities. In it, the prophet sees the high priest, Joshua, dressed in dirty clothes. Joshua stands before God, and Satan is nearby accusing him. Joshua's dirty clothing renders him ceremonially unclean and unable to fulfill his priestly duties. So, in a way, Satan has grounds for accusation. But God does not give ear to Satan's case. Instead, he rebukes Satan and instructs an angel to remove Joshua's dirty clothes. Then he says to Joshua, "Behold, I have taken your iniquity away from you" (Zechariah 3:4). Joshua is provided with fresh clothing and charged to go ahead with his God-ordained work.

As he did with Joshua, Satan accuses us in God's presence. But the same declaration of innocence made over Joshua is made over those who are in Christ.

Scripture says that God nailed our record of debts on the cross, and in doing so, "disarmed" demonic powers and "put them to open shame, by triumphing over them" (Colossians 2:14). Satan is "disarmed" because he no longer has a legal case against us. Our charges have been dismissed. Though the enemy accuses us of sin, in an amazing reversal, our Judge rebukes him instead.

While God is not moved in the least by Satan's charges, we are more easily shaken. Satan "slanders us to ourselves," writes Sibbes.[28] And though the content of Satan's accusations and the Holy Spirit's conviction may seem similar on the surface, their intent and effect are as different as life and death.

God exposes our sins to heal, but Satan does it to steal, kill, and destroy. The Holy Spirit convicts us of sin to encourage a godly grief which "produces a repentance that leads to salvation without regret" (2 Corinthians 7:10). He reminds us of who we once were so that we can rejoice in and testify to God's grace. Satan, however, induces worldly grief over our sin, leading to death. He brings up our past to *condemn* us and rob us of our confidence in Christ.

Satan even twists God's promise of justification by faith. He distorts the gospel, presenting having enough faith as a new kind of law—as if we gain salvation by believing hard enough. He highlights our doubts to make us question whether we are truly saved and then points to our lack of assurance as proof that we don't have saving faith. Just as he challenged Jesus to prove his identity, knowing full well that he was the Son of God (Matthew 4:1-11), Satan seeks to make us question whether we are truly sons and daughters of God, misusing the Scriptures to cause us to despair.

Satan not only accuses Christians of their sin and small faith; he also burdens God's people with false guilt. This is true especially for Christian perfectionists, who often more easily accept a bad word about ourselves than a good one. Writing to a woman struggling with such guilt, C.S. Lewis advised:

If there is a particular sin on your conscience, repent and confess it. If there isn't, tell the despondent devil not to be silly. You can't help hearing his voice (the odious inner radio) but you must treat it merely like a buzzing in your ears or any other irrational nuisance ... You see, one must always get back to the practical and definite. What the devil loves is that vague cloud of unspecified guilt feeling or unspecified virtue by which he lures us into despair or presumption. "Details, please?" is the answer.[29]

One reason why "Details, please?" can be helpful is that we know the Holy Spirit convicts in order to restore. To bring us to repentance, the Spirit points out very specific ways in which we need to confess, change, or make restitution. But, in my experience, it is rarely, if ever, God who is behind our general feelings of being a "bad" Christian or person.

Relentless accusations that you'll never change, or that you are lost beyond hope of rescue, are not words of truth from the Spirit who gives life. They are lies from hell, because if Satan can no longer blind you to your sins, he'll seek to highlight your sinfulness until you feel there is no help for you in Christ. Though he cannot steal your salvation, he seeks to rob you of your joy and peace. Here, you must resist the devil and cling onto Christ.

Christ is your sure hope. He sees your mustard seed of faith and says that it is enough (Luke 17:5-6). He assures you that the Father will give the Spirit to all who ask and that he graciously answers those who pray, "I believe; help my unbelief!" (Luke 11:13; Mark 9:24). He is your merciful High Priest, and he calls you to the throne of grace to find mercy in your need (Hebrews 4:16). Your faith may be weak, but he rises to defend you, and you are clothed in his righteousness.

MERCY LIKE MANNA

There is a chapter in *The Bruised Reed* titled, "Believe Christ, Not Satan." *Believe that Christ is merciful,* counsels Sibbes. Though Satan would misrepresent him to us, Jesus is ready and willing to receive sinners.

As a child, I often got stomachaches in the middle of the night.[30] I remember wanting to wake my mom but being afraid I'd get in trouble. I never got scolded for these stomachaches, but even so, I'd wait until the pain was unbearable. Then I'd tiptoe over to her and whisper so softly that she wouldn't wake up and I'd end up lying down again, still in pain. I often do the same thing with God.

I don't want to be presumptuous.

I don't want to test his patience.

I don't want to be scolded.

So I hesitate to come to him.

The enemy of my soul seeks to affirm my fears. *You're going to pray about that again? Shouldn't you be doing better by now?*

If we believe God is impatient or standing in judgment over us, we are bound to tiptoe in fear and anxiety. But consider the mercy of God, who would tell stories so that Pharisees who think they're ok but really are not might find redemption in him. Consider that he told the same stories in pursuit of sinners who would otherwise despair, and that when we feel ourselves too sinful to be received by him, he assures us that we are the very reason why he came.

Our God is rich in mercy (Ephesians 2:4). And you who have tasted this mercy need not fear its supply running low. His mercies never come to an end (Lamentations 3:22-23). Like manna, they are new every morning, for he means for you to live by them.

A PRAYER FOR WHEN YOU HEAR THE VOICE OF CONDEMNATION

God of mercy and grace,

The voices of accusation are loud right now.

I want to be righteous in your sight. But today, I'm reminded of the many ways in which I have failed to love and obey you. My sins outnumber the hairs on my head, and my heart fails within me.

God, it's hard to know which thoughts are from you, which are from me, and which are from the enemy. Quiet any thoughts that aren't from you and help me hear your voice. Deliver me from false accusations. Protect me from the evil one, who makes me feel as if I am not forgiven and will never change.

Where my conscience and the devil accuse me of sins already forgiven, let your perfect love cast out fear. You have nailed my record of debt to the cross and hurled my sins into the depths of the sea. Once for all, you have made me clean, and there is no condemnation left for me. Restore to me the joy of your salvation.

Where I am being shown ways in which I need to change, remind me that you only discipline those you love. You patiently

correct me, not in judgment but for
a harvest of righteousness and peace.
Help me not to lose heart. Empower
me to walk the way of repentance that
leads to life and leaves no regret.

Where there is no basis for these feelings
of guilt, cut through the noise and
speak truth over me. Give me grace
to endure these inward trials.

Whether I am being falsely
accused or lovingly disciplined,
turn my eyes to Christ.

In him I stand,
Clothed in righteousness
Unmerited yet forever mine.
For this I worship you,
now and all the days of my life.

In Jesus' name,
Amen

Scripture references: Psalm 40:12; Micah 7:19; Romans 8:1; Hebrews 12:7-11;
2 Corinthians 7:10

CHAPTER 4

LAW

I run in the path of your commandments,
for you have set my heart free.

PSALM 119:32 (NIV1984)

Many of my most vivid memories are of the open sky.
Like how as a child on the swings, I'd lean back as far
as my arms would allow. Tilting my head backwards so my
hair nearly brushed the floor, I'd swing, watching the clouds
and the world upside down.

Or a camping trip with family friends. We lay down on
the asphalt of an empty parking lot in the dead of night. As
we stargazed, a fireball lit up the sky, its thick tail trailing
across the expanse above us. I've haven't seen a shooting star
remotely as brilliant in the 25 years since.

And just this week, I took my kids to the park near our
house. They played by the ocean, and my son explored
rocks exposed by low tide. Water and sky before me, I
breathed deeply.

Being in these open spaces is good for my heart. The
tightness in my stomach eases a bit. The burden on my chest
too. In the goodness of creation, God gives me a taste of the
Spirit's freedom. He leads my soul to a spacious place.

A SPACIOUS PLACE

Creation's spacious places are God's grace to me because I tend to operate as if I'm walking on a tightrope. Though I know my soul is secure in an ultimate sense, it still *feels* as if I'm always just one slip away from a great fall. Psychologists call this tightrope feeling "doubts about actions," and it's a common symptom of perfectionism. You may experience it as the sensation of walking on eggshells, an incessant inner dialogue about the rightness of your choices, or paralysis in decision-making.

"Doubts about actions" is assessed in perfectionism studies with statements like:

- "I usually have doubts about the simple everyday things I do."
- "It takes me a long time to do something 'right.'"
- "Even when I do something very carefully, I often feel that it is not quite right."[31]

For the Christian perfectionist, that last statement might be reworded, "Even when *I try to obey God* very carefully, I often feel that it is not quite right." The good things we do are never good enough. We second-guess our "simple everyday" actions, afraid of inadvertently sinning. For some of us, these doubts escalate to the point of compulsive indecisiveness or a form of scrupulosity characterized as "religious OCD."

If you are burdened by constant fears over whether you are obeying God rightly, then Jesus' promise of rest is intended for you. Our good Shepherd leads us safely off our tightropes and sets our feet on spacious places.

In Psalm 18, David praises God, saying:

He brought me out into a spacious place.
  He rescued me because he delighted in me.

(Psalm 18:19, NIV)

For David, these spacious places were literal—God repeatedly delivered him from enemies and out of hiding to open safety. But these physical experiences were also used by psalmists to describe an inner reality.

Psalm 119:45 says:

I shall walk in a wide place,
  for I have sought your precepts.

Preacher Charles Spurgeon writes of this verse, "The way of holiness is not a track for slaves, but the King's highway for freemen, who are joyfully journeying from the Egypt of bondage to the Canaan of rest. God's mercies and his salvation, by teaching us to love the precepts of the word, set us at a happy rest."[32]

It may be hard to imagine, but God's law isn't meant to keep us on a never-ending tightrope walk. Through the law, God actually leads us to wide, open spaces of freedom and joy. Thus we turn now, perhaps counterintuitively, to consider how God's commands might guide us to a spacious place.

NO HIDDEN EXPECTATIONS

How can understanding the law (or commands) of God bring freedom for the Christian perfectionist? First, simply consider that God speaks. For the Christian who perpetually doubts her actions, the fact that God has spoken—and done so clearly—is solid ground.

Have you ever considered that God didn't have to say anything to us? He could have left us completely in the dark about what he's like, what he wants, and what we're here for. But he didn't stay silent. He spoke.

This is incredible to me. The gap between God's thoughts and human comprehension is as great as the distance between the heavens and the earth (Isaiah 55:9). Nevertheless, our Creator speaks in ways we can understand. Much like how an adult might use baby talk with an infant, the eternal, infinite, and holy one has accommodated us in his speech.[33] He has stooped down to speak in ways he knows we'll understand, so we don't have to be afraid of missing his voice.

God speaks through creation and his word. Through the world around us, God reveals his divinity (Psalm 19:1-6). Through his law, he revives our souls, makes us wise for salvation, and teaches us to fear him (v 7-9). And though Christians are no longer bound to the Old Testament ceremonial laws, which were fulfilled in Christ, nor to the civil laws, which only applied then to the nation of Israel, his commands still guide us today as we seek to love God and love neighbor (Matthew 22:37-40). The words of Scripture teach, rebuke, and correct us. They train us in righteousness and perfect us so that we are ready to do his will (2 Timothy 3:16-17).

As someone who is afraid of making mistakes, I find the truth that God speaks is a great comfort. It means he doesn't expect me to "just know" what is right or what he wants. Some of us know what it's like to be in a relationship or a culture that seems to require something close to mind-reading, at least from our perspective. Or we've worked under a boss whose expectations changed on a whim. It's stressful not knowing what is expected of us until *after* we fail to meet unspoken demands.

But God doesn't hold his children to hidden expectations. From the beginning, his spoken words to Adam and Eve set before them their purpose. He gave them clear instructions, spelling out the consequence for disobedience. He didn't just put them in the garden and expect them to figure it out on their own. Humanity was not meant to find our way through a game of trial-and-error, groping around in the darkness and guessing at how to live and how to please our Creator. God spoke.

Thus, the writer of Psalm 119 says, "I shall walk in a wide place, for I have sought your precepts." The whole psalm (the longest chapter in the Bible) is full of effusive praise and love for how God leads us through his law. God's commands are our delight because they are our counselors (v 24). They make us wise, teaching us to walk in the true, good way (v 98, 128). And when the road ahead of us is fraught with danger and we are afraid to walk lest we fall, his word is a lamp by our feet, revealing anything that might cause us to stumble (v 105).

God didn't have to speak, but through his precious commands, he has spoken. And those who seek him need not fear missing his voice.

THE LAW AND GOD'S HEART

If you've experienced God's merciful wounding in the conviction of sin, you may feel the need to brace yourself when approaching God's law. But God's commands do more than reveal your imperfections. They also prove his trustworthiness and his heart for you.

First, God's commands assure us that he is a safe person to trust. He is not capricious like the gods of Greek mythology, who acted out of immoral impulses and lashed out unpredictably when offended. The God of the Bible is unchanging and steadfast, and his laws reflect his character. Just as he demands his people be holy, righteous, and pure, so he is holy, righteous, and pure. Just as he calls for compassion for the helpless and needy, so God shows us compassion. Because he is perfect, he is trustworthy, and the anxious perfectionist will find him to be a steady refuge.

Second, God's commands reveal his heart for our success. I experienced a reflection of this once while taking a seminary exam. Before we began, the professor prayed something like, "God, these students have studied hard. Help them to do well." I could tell he meant it, and it moved me to think that the person who wrote and would grade my exam genuinely wanted me to succeed.

I think many Christian perfectionists subconsciously believe that God is like a harsh teacher—a mean PE instructor, maybe, with timer and clipboard in hand. He stands next to us, marking down our ineptitude as we wince at his shrill whistle. In reality, God is more like the kindergarten teacher who gives and reinforces rules for her students' learning— who rejoices in her students' successes and deeply desires that they'd flourish in her classroom.

God is not out for us to fail. His law is not meant to discourage and beat down weary believers. Far from it; he desires our success wholeheartedly. We hear this desire in God's voice after he gives the Israelites the Ten Commandments. The people promise to obey, and God says, "Oh that they had such a heart as this always ... that it might go well with them and with their descendants forever!" (Deuteronomy 5:29). Can you hear God's genuine desire that his people would obey him and know the blessing of walking in his ways?

Third, through the law, we see how God fiercely protects the true, beautiful, and good. Here we recall that a world where his rules were perfectly kept would look like the fullness of human flourishing in truth, humility, purity, justice, love, and mercy. Holding this positive vision of the law (rather than thinking of it as merely signaling what God is against) helps us remember that life with Jesus is about more than just not messing up. It is a wholehearted pursuit of truth, goodness, and beauty. The pure in heart are blessed not simply because they will avoid evil, but *because they will see God* (Matthew 5:8).

FREEDOM FROM ADD-ONS TO THE LAW

If God's commands are for our flourishing, why do Christian perfectionists often experience them as burdensome? One reason is because of human standards that we or others have added to them. We experience the weight of these add-ons to God's law when our consciences are afflicted by things that are not necessarily sinful.

If you're wondering what I mean, here is a sampling of things I've repeatedly felt guilty for:

- being proud of myself after a good parallel parking job
- not picking up garbage left by other people in a public bathroom
- not trying to share the gospel with the stranger sitting next to me on an airplane
- choosing to serve in church in a ministry that I enjoy (instead of one I don't)
- our family's choices about our kids' schooling
- falling asleep during personal Bible reading and prayer
- feeling anxious
- being self-conscious
- feeling angry

Without context, many of these examples could potentially be rooted in sin, but they also could be permissible. And that's the key here: Christian perfectionists are often plagued with guilt over *potential* sin, even where there is none.

Feelings of guilt aren't always trustworthy because our consciences aren't always reliable. They can be calloused so that we don't feel guilty when we should (Ephesians 4:18-19). Our consciences can also be overly sensitive or, in biblical terms, "weak" (Romans 14:1-4). Like the smoke alarm outside my bathroom, which is sometimes triggered by shower steam, our consciences can alert us to danger where there is none. Often, this is because our perception of God's law has been added to by ourselves or others.

Throughout the Gospels, Jesus opposed religious leaders who "tie up heavy burdens, hard to bear, and lay them on people's shoulders" (Matthew 23:4). In their interpretation and application of God's law, these leaders touted manmade regulations as divine. What was especially damaging about their rules was that they missed the heart of God's commands and instead weighed listeners down with false responsibility and guilt—all in God's name (Mark 7:1-13).

Jesus' yoke and burden stood in stark contrast to manmade laws. Instead of being hard to bear, his yoke was easy. Instead of weighing down those who tried to obey them, Jesus' commands were light. Best of all, his teaching would lead to soul rest.

Sometimes, when we are plagued with guilt and anxiety, what we most need is not forgiveness or rebuke but discernment to know whether we are carrying a yoke other than Christ's. Just as we need to discern God's conviction from Satan's accusations, we need to discern divine commands from manmade standards. We need to know what God's law really says so that our consciences can be recalibrated by God's word.[34]

LIGHTENING OUR LOADS

I once read a memoir by a woman who solo-hiked over a thousand miles on the Pacific Crest Trail. An inexperienced hiker, she overpacked and struggled on the trail with her bag (which weighed up to 70 lbs/30 kg at times) until another hiker offered help. Together, they went through her pack, talking through each item and removing non-essentials to lighten her load.[35]

What follows below is a cursory look at some types of extra-biblical rules that Christian perfectionists sometimes carry in our packs. This isn't an exhaustive list, but hopefully it will serve as a starting point as you consider whether some of your guilt stems from standards *related to* but *other than* the commands of God.

Tradition

When certain practices in our national, church, ethnic, or family cultures become strongly linked in our minds to Scripture's commands, then we can begin to treat these practices as if they are required by God rather than one of many permissible expressions of obedience.

This played out for me as I worked through "leaving and cleaving" in marriage. I'd heard prominent pastors applying this phrase from Genesis 2:24 to instruct married people to drastically minimize all interactions with and interdependence on their parents. But as a Chinese American, their advice didn't seem to apply to my situation. Limiting our family ties in the specific ways they instructed would have cut us off from valuable wisdom and help from our elders and been dishonoring to them. As a newlywed, I worried that we were disobeying God by not following these preachers' advice—until I realized their instructions were shaped more by American preferences and culture regarding the individual and the nuclear family than by biblical mandates.

Another example is the way some Christians understand "personal devotions" as something we do alone with the Bible in a quiet place. This is one way in which many believers, myself included, pray and meditate on the word of God. However, many Christians in the world don't have the luxury of time alone or even access to their own copy of the Bible. Some regularly read the Bible corporately. Many believers I know begin weekdays with early morning prayer meetings at church. Understanding the way our obedience to God's commands is influenced by church tradition helps us distinguish between a command and various permissible ways to obey it.

Personal Convictions

Our consciences can also be misinformed when we confuse personal convictions with divine commands. This is what happened with me and bathroom garbage. I'd heard about a Christian who, as part of his witness, was committed to leaving places (like his workplace bathroom) better than he found them, and I felt guilty for not doing the same.

Christians often have convictions on matters like how far to live from church, how to be involved in global missions, or where to send kids for school. These personal convictions are usually applications of a specific command from God (for example, don't neglect meeting together; make disciples of all nations; instruct your children) but they are not the *only* way to obey it. While we must find ways to live out God's commands in practical ways, we need to discern the difference between personal convictions and what Scripture requires.

Stoicism

Perfectionists can sometimes feel guilty for having negative emotions and—depending on our familial, cultural, and church upbringing—may misinterpret certain emotions as inherently wrong.[36] For example, we may be quick to moralize sadness as unbelief in God's goodness, fear as sinful worry, or anger as sinful wrath. Or we might feel guilty for feeling happy about receiving God's blessings or doing a good job, afraid of committing idolatry or of being prideful. But there are times when sadness, fear, anger, or happiness are appropriate and God-honoring. We need wisdom to know when our emotional responses are sinful and when they are permissible and God-given. Otherwise, we can inadvertently embrace stoicism (minimizing or repressing emotions) as holiness.

Asceticism

Related to stoicism, some of us tend toward asceticism— fearing desire in all forms, even ones that aren't wrong. Author Jen Pollock Michel describes this fear in *Teach Us to Want*. Regarding her desire to be a writer, she says:

> *I am a woman who has struggled long with an inordinate fear of her selfishness, a woman who has wanted a measure of certainty for finding and following the will of God. I've needed a greater reassurance that if I ever lean into my desires, I am not actually falling off a cliff.*[37]

Knowing that sins like selfishness and pride can masquerade as innocuous wants, some of us are suspicious of *all* our personal desires or ambitions, assuming they must be sinful. Christian perfectionists sometimes rely on asceticism and self-denial to make decisions—thinking that the "right" choice must always be the opposite of what we want. But godliness is not an automatic denial of all desire. Godliness means denying *sinful* desires and, at times, laying down our preferences for the sake of others. It also means pursuing God-given desires (and maybe even desires for good things that we're not sure God will grant) in faith and surrender.

Finitude

Another common mix-up is sinfulness and finitude. There is a difference between being a sinner and being limited. We have been created as embodied souls, limited in space, time, and energy. And as finite beings, we may not be able to do all the good things we wish we could do. Before being diagnosed with an autoimmune disease that explained decades of chronic pain, I felt guilty when I didn't want to do housework. I thought I was being lazy, but it turns out that I was sick.

In addition, sometimes we need reminders that making a mistake—like forgetting someone's name or missing an appointment—is not necessarily the result of a willful lack of love but of our human fallibility. Sinful error is not the same as unintentional mistakes. So while finitude and fallibility are not excuses for sin (and it's sinful to respond poorly when corrected for our mistakes!), they're not sinful in themselves.

Intrusive Thoughts

Some Christians struggle with intrusive thoughts and obsessive doubts about their spiritual lives in ways that are characteristic of "religious OCD." Counselor Mike Emlet defines this experience as:

> *Intrusive (spontaneous, unbidden, unwanted) and obsessive (persistent, recurring) thoughts and doubts about moral-spiritual issues, which produce distressing levels of anxiety and the quest to rid oneself of that anxiety, usually by one or more of the following: performing compulsive behaviors, engaging in mental rituals, or by avoiding triggering situations.* [38]

A person struggling this way experiences unwanted thoughts (e.g. "I hate God"), images (often violent, graphic, or blasphemous in nature), or impulses (e.g. feeling like cursing in church) that are spontaneous or triggered by external stimuli (e.g. by sitting in a worship service). Though these intrusive thoughts are not indicative of the true desires of the person experiencing them, they are highly distressing. Thus, to mitigate guilt and the fear that these thoughts are sinful (or indicate future sin), significant amounts of time and energy can be spent trying to suppress or resist them. A person struggling this way may end up compulsively performing behaviors or mental acts (prayer, confessing to others, repeating Bible verses, etc.) to alleviate their fear that they sinned, even when they did not. In these cases, the person will need help learning to dismiss and ignore intrusive thoughts instead of giving them more weight than they merit.

Religious OCD is complicated, and as Christian counselor Esther Smith notes in her book, *A Still and Quiet Mind:*

Twelve Strategies for Changing Unwanted Thoughts, many people have intrusive thoughts or minor compulsions without being diagnosed with OCD. OCD is "a description of a common human experience that is in its most severe form."[39] It would be impossible to address this experience fully in a few short paragraphs, so I've listed some resources in the Appendix for further reference.

Superstition

"Superstitions" are habits and beliefs that often appear spiritual but actually compel us by a fear that is disconnected from truth. They may start with a simple practice (e.g. praying for safety before you begin to drive) that morphs into the belief that if you don't do it, something bad will happen (e.g. you'll get into a car accident). Superstitions may also arise from common sayings or beliefs in our Christian communities that aren't necessarily biblical.

For example, when I was younger, I often heard "Never say never to God!" as half-joke and half-truth in personal testimonies. The implication was that if you don't want to do something (e.g. be a missionary), then God will probably make you do it. So I started deciding what ministries to serve in based on what was least appealing and most difficult, reasoning that this was how I would know God's will. I didn't realize it, but my method of discernment was a form of superstition rather than biblical wisdom.

As I've said, the list above isn't exhaustive. It is only intended to help you begin to consider whether some of your guilt and fear stems from rules that seem Christian but are actually not prescribed by God. Letting go of these standards doesn't mean you won't ever have personal convictions that you hold to, or cultural expressions of obedience required for your particular context. But it means that you will arrive at that obedience led by the Spirit in freedom and truth, and guided by God's word.[40]

Learning what obedience looks like in your life will require wisdom and practice. It will take much prayer and study of God's word. As you unload your pack, you'll also likely need help from others who've walked this way before and who thoroughly know God's grace, his commands, and you. Their wisdom and prayers will be invaluable, since it will feel scary to let go of familiar rules that you've relied on. Those struggling intensely with intrusive thoughts and compulsions may also find it helpful to see a therapist, counselor, or psychiatrist trained in treating OCD.[41]

Whatever your load, it will take time to discern what to let go of and what to keep, but Jesus is your gentle and patient Teacher. As you learn from him, you will find that his yoke is easy. His burden is light because it only includes what is essential for your flourishing.

In that hiking memoir I read, the author still had a way to go after her pack was purged. Fully loaded with supplies, it was still heavy. But compared to before? "It was so light I felt I could leap into the air."[42]

FREEDOM TO CHOOSE

Christ lovingly leads us off our tightropes into wide, spacious places of freedom. But being out in the open can come with a new set of fears. Without extra rules and regulations, how can we be certain we are obeying God? The tightrope may have been scary, but at least we knew where to step next.

Here, we need to remember that the instructions given in Scripture are actually relatively few given the multitude of choices we face every day. One of my favorite verses about obedience comes from Psalm 119: "I run in the path of your commands, for you have set my heart free" (v 32, NIV1984). Within the safeguards of the law, God grants us much liberty to choose how to love him and love our neighbors from day to day. And rather than hand us a roadmap to dictate our every step, he fills us with his Spirit and lets us run in freedom.

We take our wobbly, uncertain steps forward changed from the inside out by the word and Spirit of God, and helped along by others in God's family. We might not know where we're going, but God himself walks with us. And he will keep walking with us until we find ourselves running alongside him in the path of his commands, in a spacious place and under open skies.

A PRAYER FOR WHEN YOU FEEL LIKE YOU'RE ALWAYS DOING SOMETHING WRONG

God, who speaks,

I praise you for speaking words of rescue
and of life over me. You have made
me a new creation and filled me with
passion to walk in your ways. Yet I live
with the constant sense that I'm doing
or about to do something wrong.

You have said that if I abide in your word,
I will know the truth that sets me free.

For the ways in which I have disobeyed
your word, God, I repent.
In all else, help me walk in your freedom.

Father, help me believe that the Scriptures carry
more than rebuke for me. Let me perceive
your care, kindness, and mercy in them—
even in your commands. You don't stand
afar just waiting for me to mess up. Your
laws are proof that you want me to flourish
and that you are rooting for my obedience.

Jesus, when you were on this earth, you
fiercely opposed manmade religious
regulations, which burdened your
people. Fight for me now. I want to
learn to walk your holy way: to neither
reject your difficult commands nor

add to them. Teach me to lay aside
the sin that so easily entangles. Teach
me also to lay down the burdensome
rules I carry, which aren't from you.

Holy Spirit, my soul cries out for the
freedom that is found where you are.
Shape my conscience and surround me
with wise counselors. Guide me into all
truth so that I may live in your peace.

Rescue me because you delight in me.
Even now, lead me to a spacious place and
Set my heart free, that I may run in
the path of your commands.

Amen

Scripture references: John 8:31-32; Hebrews 12:1; 2 Corinthians 3:17

CHAPTER 5

PEACE

*There are times when a child of God, weary with
the battle of life, can say only as he lies down to rest:
"Lord, you know, we are on the same old terms."*

J. GRESHAM MACHEN

As I write, an art print—housed in a double-glass, golden frame—rests on my desk. At the center of the piece is a small illustration, drawn in black ink. A path winds through farmland toward a 1st-century Palestinian home in the distance. From this home on a hill, a set of stairs runs down to meet the path. At the bottom of the stairs, a shadowed figure is poised mid-stride.

The drawing is outlined in black, but there are touches of color too. Metallic blue, green, and golden paints highlight parts of the farm and spill into the piece's wide, empty borders. Browns and greens extend beyond the fields. A patch of silvery blue alludes to sky.

It is the painted path that draws the eye and gives the piece its name: *Prodigal Streams*. From where the darkened figure stands by the foot of the stairs, the path runs solid gold until it just about reaches the edge of the field. There, the gold turns into a river of gleaming blue. This path-turned-river pours out from the scene and flows toward the viewer. Toward me, writing at my desk—the prodigal welcomed home.

GOOD WITH GOD?

Years ago, I ran into a childhood friend I hadn't seen in a long time. After warm hellos, I pulled back from a hug, looked up at him, and asked, "Are we good?" My friend knew right away what I was referring to. Our last interaction had left me wondering if I'd offended him. So it was to my great relief that he smiled and said, "Yeah. We're good."

Christian perfectionists often carry the sense that things with God aren't good. We may frequently fight the thought, "Something is wrong with me," but at a gut level, it also feels like something is not quite right *between* us and God. I say "at a gut level" because we can believe God loves us and still feel in the day-to-day that he is unhappy with us.

In his book, *You're Only Human*, Kelly Kapic describes this feeling spot on. He writes, "Many of us experience 'God's love' as mere divine toleration."[43] Even those who believe God has forgiven them through Christ may imagine that the Father regards them with "irritable toleration."[44] As an example, Kapic asks, "Do you tend to avoid prayer because you feel like a stranger in the Father's presence rather than a safe and welcomed daughter or son?"[45]

Sometimes, as God sanctifies us, we begin to imagine that while he has much he wants to do *in* or even *through* us, he must not want very much to do *with* us—especially as we keep failing and falling. So we trust God wholeheartedly, preach him passionately, and walk in his ways zealously— all the while feeling an unease in our soul, a sense of estrangement between us and him. Beneath our service to God and our efforts to obey him, we perceive some sort of relational tension. Whether we anticipate coldness, irritability, disgust, or indifference from God, we don't expect to be fully welcomed into the divine presence. But through the stories of Scripture (and you might say *the* story of Scripture), God persistently shows us something different.

WELCOMED AND WANTED

We all carry stories that shape our conception of God. For better and for worse, our life experiences shape our understanding of words like "love," "Father," and "forgiveness." The power of Scripture's narratives is that through them, God gives us new stories to form our imaginations. Through the details that we see, hear, taste, smell, and touch in our minds' eye, we experience what God is like and how it feels to be in relationship with him. The parable of the prodigal son is one such story (Luke 15:11-32).

Here's a refresher on Jesus' parable. A son asks his dad for his share of his inheritance, leaves home, and spends all he has on reckless living. Then famine hits. Destitute, he decides he'd rather be a servant in his dad's home than starve alone, so he resolves to return, rehearsing an apology on the way back: "Father, I have sinned against heaven and before you. I am no longer worthy to be called your son. Treat me as one of your hired servants" (v 18-19).

If I'm honest, I find myself mildly annoyed at the gall of this prodigal and his apology. Why did he think it'd be a good idea to offer his services to his dad? If he knew he didn't deserve to be a son, why would he think his father would put up with the shame and humiliation of letting him join his household staff? Yet, perhaps there was more than impudence at work here. Maybe it was also the memory of the kind of person his dad was that made the son dare to hope—to think that despite all he'd done, there was a chance he'd receive mercy.

The prodigal was right to risk his return, though even he couldn't have imagined the welcome awaiting him.

It's this welcome that has been depicted so widely in art, most famously in Rembrandt's masterpiece *The Return of the Prodigal Son* and in countless other pieces like the one on my desk. It is the embrace of the father, who sees his son while he is a long way off and, abandoning all dignity, runs to him and takes him into his arms mid-apology. The intimate moment when deep vulnerability, need, and shame meet tender compassion and unimaginable grace. The prodigal is received not as a servant but as a beloved child.

The scene captures our collective imaginations because it's the turn in the story that makes us catch our breath—the ending we didn't dare to hope for but was our greatest hope all along. The lost son had hoped to find food and shelter and work. We might say that the best he could wish for was mere toleration: something between a rejection and a return to how things used to be. Instead, he finds his father's love has not waned during his time away. Rather, the opposite seems to have happened. The prodigal's lostness draws out the depth of his father's affection all the more in his compassion and yearning.

Those of us who are praying for prodigals know this yearning of love: the aching desire in our chest that they would come to their senses, no matter how far they've run. We long for their return to family, to community, to God. The 19th-century minister Horatius Bonar describes the way the father's heart goes out to the prodigal, and how it reflects the compassion of God:

> *God's hatred of the sin is not hatred of the sinner. Nay, the greatness of his sin seems rather to deepen than to lessen the divine compassion ... The farther the prodigal*

*goes into the far country, the more do the yearnings of the
father's heart go out after him in unfeigned compassion for
the wretched wanderer, in his famine, and nakedness, and
degradation, and hopeless grief.*[46]

The father's desire for his son's return and his unwavering
love for him even in his wretched wanderings explain the
unconditional and lavish welcome home.

Scripture is full of examples of this surprising welcome of
God—his invitation for sinners to draw near and his earnest
embrace of them when they do.

*Come, let us reason together. Your sins may be as crimson, but
you will be made clean* (Isaiah 1:18).

*Come, if you thirst, come to the waters. Come, buy and eat—
even if you have no money to give! Come, taste wine and milk
without price* (55:1).

*Draw near with your conscience sprinkled clean by the blood of
Christ* (Hebrews 10:22).

*Draw near to the throne of grace boldly. Find mercy and
grace to meet your need* (4:16).

Come, all who are weary and heavy laden. Receive rest
(Matthew 11:28).

This is the welcome of God for you. Your imperfections
have not consigned you to a life of being merely tolerated.
Rather, in your weakness and sin, your Father's heart goes out
to you and he says, *Come.* He isn't just seeking a change in
your behavior. He isn't even seeking your usefulness to him.
Remember that it was not extra hands for the farm that the
father longed for while the prodigal was in a distant country.
He wanted his son. So it is with your Father. In calling you to
draw near, God seeks, and has always sought, *you.*

RECONCILED FOR PEACE WITH GOD

The good news of the gospel is that through Christ, we are welcomed home and restored to God. This is where the "courtroom" image of justification that we discussed in earlier chapters reaches its limits—mainly because no one wants a deep relationship with their judge, even one who acquits them. But, as the apostle Peter writes, Christ "suffered once for sins, the righteous for the unrighteous, *that he might bring us to God*" (1 Peter 3:18). God clears us in the divine court so that, freed from sin's penalty, we can be reconciled to him. He washes away our sins so that, holy and blameless, we may enter into his presence without fear of condemnation.

Another way to put this is that Jesus died and rose again so that we could have peace with God (Romans 5:1). This is peace in a holistic sense, reflected in the Hebrew word for peace: *shalom*. Shalom doesn't just convey the absence of hostility but a sense of well-being and a restoration of things to the way they're supposed to be. This is the peace that says things between us and God are truly, unshakably good.

With God, there is no cold-shouldering, no record of wrongs kept, no subtle demand that you "earn it," no demeaning reminders of our failures. He "remembers [our] sins no more," which means he doesn't ruminate on our mistakes the same way we might (Hebrews 8:12).[47] Recollections of our wrongdoings are not simmering on his backburner as he listens to our prayers. Having paid our debt on the cross, he forgives us from his heart because his heart was always to love us and draw us to himself.

In the garden, God's first son and daughter lived at peace with him. They explored the world, asked questions, joked, rested, enjoyed one another, and tended the earth in unhindered communion with their Creator. How heartbreaking it is, then, to read Genesis 3 in light of this relationship—that the children of God would hear him walking in the garden in the cool of the day and feel the overwhelming urge to hide, instead of running toward the sound of his footsteps.

Jesus came to call us out of hiding and restore our relationship with God. We see a powerful visual of this when, upon his death, the curtain separating worshipers from the Most Holy Place in the temple was torn from top to bottom (Matthew 27:51). Through Christ, our trespasses are no longer counted against us, and our sins no longer separate us from entering into God's holy presence. We have fellowship with God (1 John 1:3).

Counselor Ed Welch has helpfully suggested that instead of thinking of Christian growth primarily as growing in holiness, it is better to think of it as "progressive nearness" to God. Our relationship with God grows deeper as we walk with him in faith and obedience. Sanctification is therefore not less than moving toward Christ-like character, but it is decidedly *more* than that. Obedience, Welch argues, is not our ultimate goal. Rather, our obedience "serves the purpose of our communion with [God]."[48]

For those of us who are hypersensitive to our faults, weakness, and sinfulness, reframing our goal as progressive nearness to God may help when we get stuck in condemnation and guilt. If drawing nearer to God is the goal, maybe we can aim to return to him a little quicker when we fall instead of staying away because we're not yet perfect. And instead of being overwhelmed by all the ways in which we still need to change, we can pursue God with excitement, knowing that there is more of him we have yet to know.

Restoration of communion—peace with God—and "progressive nearness" have always been the goal. But perhaps, like the prodigal son, the best you've dared to hope for is a life of servitude. Maybe it's barely thinkable that you'd be granted entrance into the kingdom of heaven after what you've done. It feels more than enough to no longer fear judgment after death. You can't imagine God would actually want to bring you near to himself.

So as you approach him, you begin, "Father, I have sinned against heaven and you. I'm not worthy to be your child." But hear the excited shouts of your dad as he runs to you from a distance. Feel him take you up in his arms. Before you can offer your servitude, see how you are clothed with his robe and bestowed with his ring. Savor the smells of the feast being prepared in honor of your return. This is home. This is peace with God.

WE STRIVE FROM PEACE

You are good with God, and, with joy, he invites you to draw near to him in ways it will take eternity to fully experience.

Knowing this, you may find your energy and attention shifting from rules to relationship, which is a good and necessary shift.[49] But because our perfectionistic concerns can easily transfer from our pursuit of holiness ("I'm so sinful!") to our pursuit of God ("I don't love him enough!"), we're going to camp out a bit more on another implication of being good with God—that we pursue him *from* a place of peace instead of *for* peace.[50]

Christians are called to strive. We pursue God with our all

because we know the surpassing greatness of knowing him. Having tasted communion with him, we yearn for more of it. Our hearts and flesh cry out for the living God (Psalm 84:2, NIV).

Such an earnest pursuit is good and beautiful—which is what makes it difficult when, running hard after God, we become burdened with perfectionistic concerns. Here is where we need our gentle and lowly Savior to teach us to strive from a place of peace.

The best illustration I've ever seen of the difference between striving *from* a place of peace versus striving *for* peace is in the movie *Chariots of Fire*. Based on the true story of Olympic athlete Eric Liddell, there's this great line in the film where Liddell, a Christian, says, "[God] made me fast. And when I run, I feel his pleasure." In contrast, another runner, worried about his race, says, "I'll raise my eyes and look down that corridor, four feet wide with ten lonely seconds to justify my whole existence. But will I?"

"Ten lonely seconds to justify my existence," could be the cry of Christian perfectionists, who often feel the need to earn our keep and our peace with God. It also could have described the labor of the older brother in Jesus' story—the other prodigal son, who never left his dad but toiled and toiled as his heart grew cold.

At the younger prodigal's return, a second prodigal is exposed at home. The elder son, resenting his dad's lavish welcome of his brother, refuses to join the party. He is bitter and feels shortchanged. "Look, these many years I have served you, and I never disobeyed your command," he reminds his dad (Luke 15:29). He can't understand why his work never merited even a young goat to feast on with his friends.

This son has no right to be angry at his dad's loving generosity. Yet, like his brother, he is pursued with compassion.

The dad goes after his son's heart, patiently explaining why they need to celebrate his brother's return. Then he assures him, "Son, you are always with me, and all that is mine is yours" (Luke 15:31). These are words of affirmation, not rebuke.[51] *Child, you are always with me.* Their relationship is and has always been secure. *All that is mine is yours.* He was never assessing his son's work to see if he merited an inheritance. It was already his.

The older son was meant to work the land in the context of loving relationship and deep belonging, and so are we. The apostle Paul, running hard after the call of God to know and be like Christ, wrote, "Not that I have already obtained this or am already perfect, but I press on to make it my own, because Christ Jesus has made me his own" (Philippians 3:12). Like Paul, we pursue God with passion and sacrifice *because* Jesus has already made us his.

The first question of the Heidelberg Catechism makes this clear when it asks, "What is your only comfort in life and death?" Notice how the answer places our striving in the context of belonging. The Christian's greatest comfort is:

That I am not my own,
but belong—
body and soul,
in life and in death—
to my faithful Savior, Jesus Christ.

He has fully paid for all my sins with his precious blood,
and has set me free from the tyranny of the devil.
He also watches over me in such a way

that not a hair can fall from my head
without the will of my Father in heaven;
in fact, all things must work together for my salvation.

Because I belong to him,
Christ, by his Holy Spirit,
assures me of eternal life
and makes me wholeheartedly willing and ready
from now on to live for him.[52]

We belong to our faithful Savior, who has paid for our sins and set us free from the devil's tyranny. He watches over us and knows us intimately. His Spirit assures us of eternal life, and finally, *because we belong to him,* he makes us wholeheartedly willing and ready to live for him.

Our toil and pursuit after God is meant to be undergirded by the deep relational assurance that the Lord made us and we are his (Psalm 100:3)—that, as the lover in Song of Solomon sang, "I am my beloved's and my beloved is mine." (Song of Solomon 6:3). We belong to God, body and soul, in life and in death. From this place of peace, we strive.

GOD AND USEFULNESS

One specific way in which our belonging to God pushes against the urge to justify our own existence is in challenging our ideas of usefulness. One of my great fears, tied to guilt and shame, used to be that I was too sinful ever to be used by God. "What if God won't use me?" I once asked a mentor who, in God's grace and wisdom, didn't assure me of my great usefulness. He didn't even say that God would forgive, change, and *then* use me. Instead he asked, "What if that's not the right question?"

In his piece, "On Living"—written for those struggling with despair and hopelessness—author Alan Noble notes that though the world, the flesh, and the devil measure the worth of our lives by "usefulness," God sees things differently:

> *Usefulness is the sole criterion for the World, the Flesh, or the Devil. But you have no use value to God. You can't. There is nothing He needs. You can't cease being useful to God because **you were never useful to begin with**. That's simply not why He created you and why He continues to sustain your being in the world. ... He made us just because He loves us and for His own good pleasure. Every other reason to live demands that you remain useful, and one day your use will run out. But not so with God. To God, your existence in His universe is an act of creation, and it remains good **as** creation even in its fallen state.*[53]

Noble is not saying that we're useless in the sense of being worthless or incapable of doing any good. We each have a purpose here on earth, and God has prepared good works for us to do (Ephesians 2:10). But even as we do these good works, we need to know that they are not needed in order to affirm the inherent goodness of our lives. We are loved and sustained by God apart from our so-called "usefulness" to him.

Knowing we were made in love for God's good pleasure changes the way we work. In God's home, you don't have to earn your keep or prove you deserve your place. Created, redeemed, sustained, cared for, and welcomed into his presence simply out of his love, you do not need to justify your own existence. Thus you can serve and strive, not *for* but *from* a sense of freedom, belonging, and peace. You "run" in the light of God's good pleasure.

I needed my mentor to question my question regarding God using me because behind it was more than an earnest desire to serve God. Alongside a deep fear of my own sinfulness was a core belief that I needed to justify my existence through my usefulness to God. But there is, in the words of Jesus, a better portion (Luke 10:42)—a greater priority for my life than my service to him: being with him, known and loved, and knowing and loving him in return.

THE SAME OLD TERMS

Though we are at peace with God, there will be times when we have trouble feeling his peace. It might be because we are being disciplined and still feel the sting of correction. Or God may feel far away because our bodies are faltering due to physical pain, tiredness, or mental illness. Sometimes we won't know exactly why.

Our feelings matter to God. Whether they are feelings of estrangement, anxiety, or sadness in our relationship with him, he cares. But we also have assurance that even when we sense our closeness with God waning, his heart for us is unfaltering and unchanging—that we are at peace with him, even when we don't feel that peace subjectively in our own hearts. "There are times," writes theologian J. Gresham Machen, "when a child of God, weary with the battle of life, can say only as he [or she] lies down to rest: 'Lord, you know, we are on the same old terms.'"[54]

So pray to feel his peace, and ask others to pray for you as well. Just as the father of the older prodigal said, *Child, you are always with me*, your Father is happy to reassure you of your place with him as much as you need. He truly does want your heart to find rest in him because he cares for you. But as you wait for the peace that transcends understanding, remember that nothing you do or don't do, or feel or don't feel, will change his heart for you.

You are good with God. You belong to him. Welcomed home, you are always with him, and all he has is yours (1 Corinthians 3:21–22).

A PRAYER FOR WHEN YOU'RE AFRAID TO PRAY

King of kings, Lord of lords,

I give you honor and praise. For though
you dwell in a high and holy place,
you are close to the brokenhearted and
save those who are crushed in spirit.

I confess that I sometimes still feel like a
prodigal, even though I've come home.
I doubt your goodness, wander from
your ways, and don't feel worthy to
be called your child. So I try my best
to obey you with my head down. In
fear of your disapproval, I keep my
distance. But you are not far from me.

Father, with compassion, you sought me
in a distant land and brought me near
by the blood of Christ. Thank you for
not being ashamed to run after me.

Jesus, you are the elder brother who
welcomed me back with great joy.
Even now, you watch over me
with care, and I belong to you.

Holy Spirit, continue to assure
me of this belonging.

Lifter of my head, you have given
me a better story than one where
I am merely tolerated.

Teach me what it means to belong to
this household where I am always
wanted and always welcome.

Reassure me day by day of my
place here at peace with you.

Whether in praise, thanksgiving, or
intercession, let me be quick to
run to your throne of grace.

Remind me that there, I will find
abounding mercy and loving welcome
in the presence of my Father.

In Jesus' name,
Amen

Scripture references: Isaiah 57:15; Psalm 34:18; Ephesians 2:13; Hebrews 4:16

CHAPTER 6

PATIENCE

A little grace, a spark of true love to God, a grain
of living faith, though small as mustard-seed,
is worth a thousand worlds.

JOHN NEWTON

The kids were late to school today—and though I scolded one of them for reading at the kitchen counter instead of helping everyone get ready to go, really it was my fault. The problem was that throughout the whole mad morning rush, I'd assumed that thermos lunches and air-fried tater tots and feet wearing both shoes *and* socks would come together faster than they did.

I don't know why I'm constantly surprised that, in the words of poet Mary Oliver, "Things take the time they take," but I am.[55] I am often perplexed at the time-taking nature of things like cooking meals and getting out the door and raising children and being sanctified.

A LENGTHENING PERSPECTIVE

That sanctification takes time means I'm not yet who I'm supposed to be. Progress toward Christ-likeness is painfully slow, and as my self-directed frustration mounts, I often assume that God is just as impatient with me as I am with myself. But he is not like me, and I greatly need his lengthening perspective.

The theologian B.B. Warfield wrote of this "lengthening perspective" in his book *Studies in Perfectionism*. In it, Warfield examines a theological error that was also known as "Christian perfectionism"—although the term meant something different to him than the way we've been using it. Warfield was describing the false teaching that Christians could achieve sinless perfection in this life. Of those who taught this error, he wrote:

> *They ask to be themselves made glorified saints in the twinkling of an eye. God's ways are not their ways, and it is a great trial to them that God will not walk in their ways. They ... adjust themselves with difficulty to the lengthening perspective of God's gracious working.*[56]

These teachers, writes Warfield, can't understand why God's work would take time. They expect perfection now, when they actually need the "lengthening perspective" of sanctification. Many of us could use the same change of perspective.

A ministry leader once told me that I needed to accept the fact that I was going to sin every day for the rest of my life. His pointedness caught me off guard but was also surprisingly helpful. Part of the reason I was finding it hard to move on from guilt and shame, even after repenting, was my expectation that I should be perfect already.

Jesus himself set our expectations when he taught his disciples to pray, "Forgive us our sins."[57] That God wants us to pray this way affirms that, as the Reformer Martin Luther wrote, the whole Christian life is to be one of repentance.[58] Jesus knew that we would need to pray regularly for forgiveness because we would regularly sin. Though God can turn water to wine in an instant, he usually chooses to make the best wine through the best grapes, grown through the consistent labor of learned vinedressers, generations of expertise, and the passing of many days.[59] In the same way, true compassion, humility, trust, patience in affliction, and godliness are cultivated over a lifetime of suffering and trial, of failing and repenting and receiving grace to get up again. "Learn from me," Jesus said (Matthew 11:29). And apparently, learning takes time.

THE NARRATIVES

Acknowledging that growth in righteousness is a lifelong process and that God knows this, the next thing we might consider is how God deals with us as in-process people. Thankfully, we have plenty of examples of how God deals with those still being sanctified because, as we'll see, our forerunners in the faith were faithful but broken, like us.

Like a deposit of precious mineral, the rich vein of God's patience runs through our story as his people. We have the patriarchs of the Old Testament, whom God was pleased to identify with as "the God of Abraham, Isaac and Jacob" (Exodus 3:16, NIV). These men were full of faith but also of cowardice, unbelief, and swindling. We have Moses, who led God's complaining people out of Egypt but gave in to complaining and anger himself. We have a prophet who was overtaken by bitterness and anger (Jonah) and judges whose lives were wrecked by their lust (Samson) and rashness (Jephthah). Even Elijah, we're told, was a man with a sinful nature just like us (James 5:17)

Yet through these Old Testament stories, we see God's grace, compassion, patience, and steadfast love. He kept his promises to the patriarchs despite their faithlessness. He sustained

Moses and the Israelites in the wilderness. He pursued wayward Jonah with a storm and his word. He answered the prayers of sinners like Samson, Jephthah, and Elijah.

In the New Testament, we have the disciples literally walking with God in flesh and still doing and saying foolish things. Reading their stories, it can feel as if Jesus is hanging out with a group of little kids. They bicker about which of them is the greatest, fight for the best seat in glory, and are embarrassingly slow to understand things Jesus repeatedly teaches. Yet reading the Gospels, you never get the feeling that Jesus is losing it with them. There are times when he is grieved and upset at their lack of faith but not in a way that causes him to demean or belittle them, or give up on them in exasperation. Instead, he teaches, corrects and affirms them and walks with them to the very end as they imperfectly follow him.

I find particular comfort in Peter, as I think many people do. My husband identifies with him as the disciple who always put his foot in his mouth. I identify with his mixture of earnest zeal and prideful overestimation of himself. He asks Jesus to call him out of the boat to walk on water but immediately gets intimidated by the waves (Matthew 14:22-32). He declares that Jesus is the Christ but is used by Satan to try to keep Jesus from the cross (16:13-23). He won't let Jesus wash his feet but then overcorrects and tells him to wash his whole body (John 13:6-11). And in the presence of his friends, he declares that even if *they* all deserted their Teacher, *he* never would—only to deny even knowing Jesus when courage and allegiance are most critical (Mark 14:29-31, 66-72).

Peter so often gets it wrong. But how does Jesus respond?

When Peter says, "Depart from me, for I am a sinful man," Jesus tells him not to be afraid—and, despite the many ways in which Peter still must change and grow, Jesus promises to make him a fisher of men, and later, a rock and pillar of the church (Luke 5:8-11; Matthew 16:18).

When Peter declares, "You shall never wash my feet!" Jesus corrects him. Then he kneels to clean and wipe Peter's dirty feet.

And after Peter's bitter betrayal, Jesus cooks him breakfast (John 21:1-19). On a shore by a lake, the resurrected Christ tends a charcoal fire with fish and bread for his friends. Having fed Peter, Jesus gives him an opportunity to reaffirm his love, casting his call once more to this fisher of men: *I know you failed, but feed my sheep. Follow me.*

Regarding Jesus' closest friends, preacher Martyn Lloyd-Jones once said, "I never cease to be grateful to these disciples. I am grateful to them for every mistake they ever made, for every blunder they ever committed, because I see myself in them."[60] Their stories are an invaluable gift to us, written down so that we might see ourselves in them and, what's more, see God's patience with people like us.

THE SURPRISING PATIENCE OF GOD

"Wonderful is the patience of the Lord, who can bear with us all at once!" writes John Newton. "We, alas, can hardly bear with each other one at a time."[61] Newton makes a case here for what I think is one of the biggest reasons why we find it so hard to think of God as patient. His patience surprises us because of how unlike us he is.

Perhaps we assume God must be impatient with us because his standards are so high: that because he is holy and wise, he isn't one to suffer fools. *New York Times* op-ed contributor

David Brooks responded once to an article that profiled someone as not "suffering fools gladly":

> *The phrase is often used as an ambiguous compliment. It suggests that a person is so smart he has trouble tolerating people who are far below his own high standards. It is used to describe a person who is so passionately committed to a vital cause that he doesn't have time for social niceties toward those idiots who stand in its way. It is used to suggest a level of social courage; a person who has the guts to tell idiots what he really thinks.*
>
> *Sure, it would be better if such people were nicer to those around them, the phrase implies, but this is a forgivable sin in one so talented ... This sounds fine in the abstract, but when you actually witness somebody in the act of not suffering fools gladly, it looks rotten.*[62]

Brooks goes on to describe watching a senior Congressman "rip into" a young reporter for asking an ill-informed question. And I'm struck at how true it is that we expect those who are great in the world to be easily provoked at their lessers.

It isn't just politicians, celebrities, or sports stars. In my sinful nature, I am also more apt to lose my patience when I feel someone is less powerful, capable, smart, or good than me. So I assume that God must likewise be annoyed by my constant stumbling—that irritation rises in him as I return to him once more for forgiveness.

But God is not like me. He is different than the "great" in this world who are harsh toward those who are less smart or rich or beautiful or morally pure. Jesus assures the weary and heavy laden that as we learn from him, he is gentle with us (Matthew 11:29). His gentleness is not weakness but meekness—strength under control.

On this, Puritan pastor Stephen Charnock wrote:

Men that are great in the world are quick in passion, and are not so ready to forgive an injury, or bear with an offender, as one of a meaner rank. It is a want [i.e. lack] of power over that man's self that makes him do unbecoming things upon a provocation. A prince that can bridle his passions is a king over himself as well as over his subjects. God is slow to anger because [he is] great in power. He hath no less power over Himself than over His creatures: he can sustain great injuries without an immediate and quick revenge: he hath a power of patience, as well as a power of justice.[63]

God is "king over himself," and with perfect mastery over himself at all times, he exercises his power accordingly. Though he outranks us to the highest degree, he never suffers from unplanned outbursts or uncontrolled irritation toward us. Rather, his "wisdom and will is pleased to act with a stateliness and sobriety which becomes His exalted majesty."[64] He always conducts himself in a way that is fitting for one who is exalted and holy.

In 1 Thessalonians, the apostle Paul commands church leaders to do the same. They are to admonish the idle, encourage the fainthearted, and help the weak, while being *patient with them all* (5:14). One key to this patience may be tucked into his benediction a few verses later: God himself will sanctify his people completely, keeping them blameless at his coming. Knowing this, church leaders can trust God with their people's progress. With confidence, Paul says, "He who calls you is faithful; he will surely do it" (v 23-24).

When helping others in their relationship with God, I often have to fight the impulse to be impatient. To expect them to get it right—and get it right *now*. I am powerless to convict someone of sin. I can't force a loved one to make right choices. I am unable to change hearts.

So I panic.

In fear, I resort to speaking sharply. I use words to shame. Or I sigh in frustration and withdraw, temporarily giving up all hope for their change. This is me frenetically depending on fleshly power to try to bring about God's will. But these methods don't lead to lasting change and only expose my sinful impatience. This is true when I'm seeking to change another person. It's just as true when the person I hope to change is myself.

But God doesn't wonder if things will end up going the way he wants with those he loves and knows. (Remember how he told Peter he'd make him a fisher of men and a pillar of the church—*and then did it?*) He doesn't panic. He doesn't need to resort to motivating us via fleshly impatience. Rather, perfect in power, he accomplishes his will in all things. He sanctifies us in his time, admonishing, encouraging, and helping—powerful and patient with us all.

REJOICE IN PROGRESS

Here's another comforting way in which God is different than us. Perfectionists tend to have selective attention. We often overgeneralize (e.g. one mistake means I am a failure) or have black-and-white thinking (e.g. one error in a project means the whole thing is bad). We also tend to pay attention to the negatives while discounting or minimizing the positives.[65]

This means that more often than not, Christian perfectionists struggle to see the good that God is doing in us. Even if we are not harboring secret or willful sins, often all we can see in ourselves is our remaining pride, selfishness, impatience, fear of people, or lack of love. God, however, always sees the whole picture, and he delights in our growth and progress.

Often, it's godly leaders who are afflicted by this perfectionistic thinking. These are men and women of character, integrity, and demonstrable fruit of the Spirit. But because they are sensitive to their remaining sin, they wonder if they ought to relegate themselves to the sidelines in the church, even as those who know them assure them otherwise. If this is you, be encouraged by Paul's exhortation to Timothy to live in a way "that all may see your progress" (1 Timothy 4:15). Paul's (and God's) expectation for this young church leader was not perfection but growth. Though Timothy still had room to mature, the community of God would be helped as they witnessed his progress in real time.

For all Christians, leaders or not, true change only comes by God's supernatural grace. Thus, the smallest evidence of trust in God, of endurance under trial, of good work done out of love—our progress in the faith—is worth noticing and celebrating.

Consider Jesus' words to the churches in Revelation. John's vision opens with Jesus addressing seven 1st-century churches situated in cities still located within present-day Turkey. Most of these churches are in need of serious correction (which Jesus gives). Nevertheless, Jesus still publicly commends what is good in them.[66] To the church who has abandoned their first love, Jesus says he knows their toil and patient endurance for his name's sake (Revelation 2:2-3). To the church sinfully putting up with false teaching, he says that he knows they dwell "where Satan's throne is" and yet hold fast to Jesus' name (v 13). To the church wrongly tolerating a seductive false prophetess, he says he knows their works, love, faith, service, and endurance (v 19). And so on.

These are real encouragements from Jesus. He understands how difficult it has been for these believers to keep the faith and recognizes they are still holding on. He has words of correction, yes, but also words of praise. Even as he tells them to repent, he encourages them to persevere by calling attention to the good he sees in them. He does the same for you.

When our family had a foster child living with us who had severe developmental delays, we experienced each milestone he hit—eating solids, crawling, saying "no"—as a hard-won, miraculous answer to prayer. Each victory was recognized and celebrated by family members, church friends, and even social workers. In the same way, perhaps we'd be less hesitant to celebrate who we are today if we remembered that even the tiniest spark of spiritual growth in our lives is a miracle. If we took time to really think about who we would be apart from God and to consider the difference Jesus has made, we'd be in awe of how far we've come.

What is the difference Jesus has made? I'm not talking about comparing today with yesterday or last week, but about looking back months, years, and decades. How are you different because of his long-term work in you? With this lengthened perspective, can you see the ways in which God has changed you?[67] If so, rejoice with him in your progress, even as you pursue him all the more.

WHY IT TAKES A LONG TIME
Counselor David Powlison has compared sanctification to walking up the stairs with a yo-yo. Hour to hour and day to

day, we may feel like we're going up and down, but in the long-run, there is progress.[68] But why this yo-yo-ing when God could just perfect us in the blink of an eye? I think of how one of my kids used to protest when waiting. She'd complain in toddler-speak, "Why it takes a long time?"

This question was at the heart of the despair that descended on me during that prolonged season of the Spirit's conviction in college. Depression isn't always tied to spiritual issues, but at the time, the question of purpose was a lynchpin for me. "What is the point of living," I wondered, "if I'm just going to sin every day?"[69]

God answered me during a campus prayer gathering. I remember sitting on the floor, back against the wall of a large meeting room above the dining hall. I remember the sentence that entered my mind, unbidden. Even more, I remember the way the persistent darkness lifted in a moment.

The key word spoken to me was "glory." In that word, God demolished my unspoken belief that the only life worth living was one in which I was perfect. I was still alive because somehow it brought him glory for me to be here, even in my sinfulness, and for now, that would be enough.

Pastor John Piper has said that the greatest threat to his faith, the reason why he is most likely to doubt his salvation or the power of the Holy Spirit, is the slowness of his sanctification. Yet, "since the Bible portrays it as a process, God must in the big picture, get more glory through the process."[70] In his wisdom, God has chosen to sanctify us over time. This means that, somehow, it brings him glory for us to remain on earth even as we inevitably sin as we're being perfected.

We've already touched on how God created us in his good pleasure. Our very existence as created beings brings him glory as our Creator and Sustainer, even in our fallen state. But exactly why it brings God glory for our sanctification to be a process is in many ways a mystery. For now, the answer is beyond the limits of our own understanding, so we are called to rest in his good purposes. If God is content to change us over time and is patient with us as he does so, we can be content to trust in his ways, even though we don't understand them fully.

And while we don't know God's full purposes behind sanctifying us over time, we do see one way in which he glorifies himself in the process. In the same letter where he instructs Timothy to let everyone see his progress, Paul writes of his own conversion. He says that although he was the worst of sinners, he received mercy so that "Jesus Christ might display his perfect patience as an example to those who were to believe in him for eternal life" (1 Timothy 1:16).

Paul saw his own story of sinfulness and salvation as a way in which others could come to see God's *perfect patience* and believe. As Christians, we need inspiring examples of faith, obedience, and sacrifice. But we also need stories of failure and redemption to give us hope— stories that show God's patience with sinners. In the poem I quoted at the beginning of this chapter, "Don't Worry," Mary Oliver refers to one such story: about a 5th-century bishop in north Africa named Augustine. Augustine's account of his own long and winding journey of faith has lit the way for spiritual wanderers for over 1,600 years. His most famous work, *Confessions*, recounts his sins (before and *after* conversion), his searching, and God's grace. Precisely because of the time it took Augustine to, as Oliver puts it, "become Saint Augustine," his story still invites the restless to find rest in God today.[71]

Could it be that God is also writing such stories in our lives? Of winding roads and restless hearts. Of progress and his wonderful patience through it all. So that through our brokenness, another child of God might look at us and say, "If God was so patient with her, and if he has changed her and is changing her, there is hope for me yet."

IN HIS TIME

I often think of the Gothic cathedrals in Europe when I find myself impatient about the way things work in God's kingdom. The Duomo in Milan (the city of Augustine's conversion) took almost six centuries to build. Paris's Notre Dame took 200 years, and the Cologne Cathedral over 600. Their designers did not expect to see their work finished in their lifetimes. It is said that when architect Antoni Gaudí was criticized about the construction time of Spain's Sagrada Família, he responded, "My client is not in a hurry."

Though much is left undone in us, God is not in a hurry. In what we feel to be the repetitive, cyclical nature of our being disciplined and growing and falling and returning, he is accomplishing his eternal work. And if he is patient with us in our starts and stops, our slow progress and falls, maybe we can learn to be patient with ourselves too.

As you pursue him, you will need both zeal and patience, especially when your sanctification feels slow. Do not worry. Things take the time they take because God is making all things beautiful in his time (Ecclesiastes 3:11). Pay attention and you'll catch glimpses of this beauty now, in your progress, which is worth a thousand worlds.

A PRAYER FOR WHEN ALL YOU CAN SEE ARE YOUR FAILURES

God of hope,

You have brought me out of darkness
to declare your praises, yet I am
struggling to walk in your light.

It feels like every step I take toward
you, I stumble ten steps back. My
growth in love and holiness has
been so slow. I am losing hope.

Hear my cry, O God.
Listen to my prayer.
When my heart is overwhelmed, lead
me to the rock that is higher than I.

Father, if you kept a record of sins, who
could stand? But with you there is
forgiveness. Because you are perfect
in all your ways, you deal patiently
with me. Thank you for standing ever
ready to receive and forgive me.

Jesus, in your perfection, you have never
despised sinners. Because of your
death and resurrection, my old self has
died, and I am a new creation. You
call me one of your holy ones. Help
me remember who you say I am.

Holy Spirit, I praise you for the good work
you are doing in me. Because you dwell
in me, I resist sin, obey your commands,
and love others in ways I never would
have before. Fill me with joy and peace
that I might overflow with hope.

Eternal God, a thousand years are but
a watch in the night for you. You are
not panicking as you accomplish your
will on earth or in me. Your ways and
thoughts are higher than mine. So if it
brings you glory for me to live as a work
in progress, I submit to your purposes.
Make me a testimony of your perfect
patience for others who need hope.

In Jesus' name,
Amen

---

*Scripture references: 1 Peter 2:9; Psalm 61:1; Psalm 130:4; 2 Corinthians 5:17;
Romans 15:13; Psalm 90:4; Isaiah 55:8-9*

CHAPTER 7

PROVIDENCE

Grace is the good news of unfathomable possibility.

JAMES K.A. SMITH

"Every day you wake up in a world that you didn't make. Rejoice and be glad," writes author Jonathan Rogers, and today I wake up to a glorious fall day on the East Coast.[72] On a short drive to the kids' school, I pass more hues of reds, oranges, and golds than I know how to name. *Orange-pink*, suggests my daughter for the dogwood tree on the front lawn. All this gratuitous beauty, and my eyes get to feast on it.

This beauty is personal—divine intent lies behind every shade of these ombré trees. My God is not a distant deity who has wound the clock, visited for a few important moments of history, and left me to live out my days alone until he returns for judgment. No, he is nearer to me than my own breath. Even now, he upholds the universe and my very being with his word. His care is not algorithmic. It is personal and real and everywhere, and sometimes what I need most is his help to recognize it, even as I receive it. "I know you love me; help me see and feel it," I've sometimes prayed.

Mercy and goodness pursue us in thousands of ways all around if we have eyes to see it. Each fall leaf is evidence that God is near.

RUBE GOLDBERG

The practice of paying attention to the world around me pushes against the tendency I have as a perfectionist to overestimate my own power and responsibility. If God clothes the lilies and feeds the sparrows, and not one strand of my hair falls without his accounting, I don't have to carry the weight of the world on my shoulders (Matthew 6:26-30; Luke 12:7).

When considering past regrets or decisions about the future, we Christian perfectionists often see our choices as a kind of trigger for a Rube Goldberg machine. You may have seen such a contraption before in a museum, movie, or online video. They're made of a series of simple mechanical processes that come together in complicated and amusing ways. Maybe a marble rolls down a ramp into a line of dominos which trigger an alarm that releases a swinging bowling ball, and so on, until—surprise!—a cup of lemonade is served or a piece of toast pops up and is slathered with jam.

For the Christian perfectionist, though, the chain reaction takes a darker turn.[73] Instead of a cup of lemonade or a delightful piece of toast, we often imagine our actions leading to a cascade of destruction and harm. We fear being less than perfect because we are haunted by the thought that we, and others, will reap the consequences of our sins and failures. We know we are responsible for making choices that have consequences in this lifetime and beyond, and this burden weighs heavily on us.

Our fears are understandable given that the principle of reaping what we sow is taught in Scripture (Galatians 6:7-9). God designed the world so that our choices reverberate into the future in seen and unseen ways, and much of the Bible lays this before us starkly. Timely words bring healing to others (Proverbs 12:18). Trust in God leads to safety (29:25). Labor yields profits (14:23). On the flip side, selfish choices lead to broken relationships (James 3:16), harsh words to deep wounds (Proverbs 12:18), lying to destruction (Psalm 5:6), and fear of man to entrapment (Proverbs 29:25).

Scripture encourages us to consider the outcomes that follow disobedience and foolishness so that we make wise choices. But for the Christian perfectionist, these considerations are endless and relentless. They fill us with anxiety and regret as we wonder:

- "What if my coworker never hears the gospel because I never shared it with him before he changed jobs?"
- "What if God won't bless the ministry I'm involved with in church because I'm not humble enough yet?"
- "What if I take this job and end up missing God's purpose for my life?"
- "What if I don't confront this person about her sin and she ends up falling away from Jesus and it's my fault?"
- "What if my friend never wants to go to church again because I said the wrong thing?"

Rube Goldberg machines are fun to watch but extremely burdensome to live. There is a kind of fatalism with them—an inevitability once the ball starts rolling—because they are set up to work without intervention. But the good news for us is that God did not set up the world and leave it. And he is not watching from the stands as our lives play out as a series of impersonal chain reactions. Though there are real-life consequences to our decisions to obey or disobey God, the Bible teaches that our Creator is actively involved in our days, directing our lives and history's every ebb and flow with wisdom and grace.

There is a power at work in the world much greater than me and my choices. God is working, and the weary Christian perfectionist can rest in the knowledge of his gracious providence.

COMPLETELY IN GOD'S HAND

Put simply, God's providence is his power over everything so that all things happen according to his will.[74] This all-encompassing language might sound abstract, but providence is as concrete as fall weather, orange-pink leaves, and our very tangible mistakes and sins. As the Heidelberg Catechism puts it, God's providence is…

> *the almighty and ever present power of God*
> > *by which God upholds, as with his hand,*
> > > *heaven*
> > > *and earth*
> > > *and all creatures,*
> > *and so rules them that*
> > > *leaf and blade,*
> > > *rain and drought,*
> > > *fruitful and lean years,*
> > > *food and drink,*
> > > *health and sickness,*
> > *prosperity and poverty—*
> > *all things, in fact,*
> > *come to us*
> > > *not by chance*
> > > *but by his fatherly hand.*[75]

The Bible says that *everything* happens because of God's will (Ephesians 1:11). From the smallest detail in our lives to the most significant events in world history, "all things, in fact, come to us not by chance." God actively upholds all created things by his power (Hebrews 1:3). He rules the fall of sparrows and the falling of rain, the rising and setting of the sun, and the rise and ruin of kings (Matthew 10:29; 5:45; Psalm 2). From him come our best days as well as our worst (Ecclesiastes 7:14). Life and death are inescapably dealt to all by him (Deuteronomy 32:39).

Not only is God's providence universal; it is also personal. He rules over and orders all things as our loving Father. All things come to us "by his fatherly hand." This means that for those who love and have been called by God, "all things work together for good" (Romans 8:28).

We need this big view of God's power and care when we're hounded by past regrets, paralyzed by present choices, and afraid about future failures. Because, though Scripture affirms both human responsibility and God's providence as equally real, they are not equal in influence. The Christian's future is not ultimately determined by her own power to always know and do what is right but by the gracious providence of God.

HE LEADS

As we seek to walk in righteousness and holiness, or face decisions with no obvious right choices, we can take comfort in knowing that God's providence means he is able to lead us where he wants us to go.

Much of my anxiety as a younger Christian stemmed from a deep desire to know and do God's will. I feared that I'd miss it somehow. My fears came from an earnest heart to please God. They were also shaped in part by a sense of self-determination. I saw my choices as the major determiners of my future, forgetting that I hadn't gotten to the place of decision on my own. Any crossroad I stood at, I'd been led to.

Recently, my daughter saw a family photo taken before she was born. "Where was I?" she asked, before remembering our usual answer to this question: "God was thinking of me?" We've taught her this not just to placate her but because it's true. The apostle Paul writes that God chose us in Christ "before the foundation of the world" (Ephesians 1:4), and that he did this "according to the purpose of his will" and "to the praise of his glorious grace" (v 5-6). Even before he made the world, God was thinking of you and determined to save you in Christ.

When standing at a point of decision that seems to dictate the course of your life with God, take comfort in knowing that you did not orchestrate your birthplace or birthdate, the Christians you'd encounter, or the way you'd hear the gospel. *God* did in his wonderful, gracious will. Before you knew him, he chose you. Before you knew to seek him, he sought you. Your salvation is founded upon his gracious providence. And if he was able to accomplish his will in your life even when you weren't looking for him, how much more can you trust him to guide you as you seek to obey him now?

The missionary Elisabeth Elliot has written, "Does it make sense to believe that the Shepherd would care less about getting His sheep where He wants them to go than they care about getting there?"[76] This thought has often brought me great comfort—that as much as I want to follow God, he is even more keen on making sure I am following. Knowing he is committed to leading me, I can make choices with confidence that "the LORD will fulfill his purpose for me" (Psalm 138:8).

Not only does God lead us, but his providence is also our hope when we miss the way of obedience. For anyone who has ever missed or fears missing the way, theologian J.I. Packer writes:

> *If I found I had driven into a bog, I should know I had missed the road. But this knowledge would not be of much comfort if I then had to stand helpless watching the car sink and vanish; the damage would be done, and that would be that. Is it the same when a Christian wakes up to the fact that he has missed God's guidance and taken the wrong way? Is the damage irrevocable? Must he now be put off course for life? Thank God, no. Our God is a God who not merely restores, but takes up our mistakes and follies into his plan for us and brings good out of them.*
>
> *This is part of the wonder of his gracious sovereignty ... God makes not only the wrath of man to turn to his praise but the misadventures of Christians too.*[77]

Knowing that God is able to turn the misadventures of Christians to his praise helps me to, as one of my ministry leaders used to say, "do the next best thing" after I've missed the way of obedience. Instead of standing in the bog, I can confess and receive forgiveness where needed, and then rise and take the next step. I have hope knowing that though I've gone the wrong way, God graciously corrects my course. Just as a GPS is able to bring me to my final destination despite missed turns, he will make sure that I make it to where he wants me to be.

WHAT WE MEAN FOR EVIL OR GOOD

Sometimes, my fear and dread of making mistakes is rooted in the sense that my imperfections will hurt those around me. In communal cultures especially (like my own), we are taught to instinctively consider the way our every decision affects those around us. Success and failure are not just matters concerning the individual but the good of the whole. This awareness of interdependence in our culture shapes the nature of our perfectionistic concerns.[78]

While some cultures may stress interdependence more than others, the Bible teaches a radical communal identity for believers of all types and backgrounds. We were created to need and be needed by others. As Christians we have been made part of one body—the church of Jesus Christ—so we rejoice together when one part rejoices and hurt together when one part is hurting (1 Corinthians 12:26).

Our actions profoundly affect other people—which is why my church's weekly prayer of repentance includes the confession that "we have not fully loved our neighbors as ourselves."[79] One way to think of sin is as a curving into oneself (to borrow an image from Augustine)—and, since we are communal beings, this inward turn leads to collateral damage. Our anger spills from our hearts and wounds others through our biting words (Galatians 5:15). Our bitterness can grow and spread to cause trouble for many (Hebrews 12:15). Our cowardice and apathy perpetuate injustice (Isaiah 58). Our failure to back up well-wishing with tangible help means others suffer (James 2:15-16). Knowing these things, Christian perfectionists often fear the ripple effects of, as the confession at my church puts it, "what we have done and left undone."[80]

My attentiveness to all I've left undone explains the perennial sense of regret I feel whenever I leave somewhere or something. Whether it's leaving a ministry, transitioning into a new season of home life, saying goodbye to someone who's leaving our church, or simply ending a conversation, I'm often thinking of all the opportunities I missed to love well. I could always have sacrificed a bit more, given more freely of myself, or listened and loved better.

Regret looks back, but fear looks ahead, and I become anxious when serving others. I fear my distractedness or self-centeredness or lack of wholehearted spiritual preparation will affect those I lead in worship. I fear my failure to pray enough for the high-schoolers I teach in Sunday school means they will fall away from God. I fear that others will misunderstand God because of my imperfect representation of him.

My fears aren't completely baseless. Years after graduation, a high-school friend told me that she had been turned off from Christianity *because of me*. I had shared the gospel with her, but I also unknowingly hurt her in our friendship. For various reasons, she saw me as a hypocrite and didn't want anything to do with my faith.

Perhaps you've had similar experiences. You've seen the way in which your sins have impacted others, so you are extra cautious now, constantly second-guessing and re-evaluating your actions, maybe wary of even trying to do good for fear of inadvertently causing harm. When plagued by such regrets and fears, I've found the story of Joseph a great help.

At the end of Genesis, Joseph is standing before his brothers, who'd sold him into slavery. They'd sold him in jealousy and hatred, but through the long narrative of slavery, wrongful imprisonment, and forgottenness, God was accomplishing his plan in Joseph's life. God had purposed for Joseph to rise to power in Egypt. Not only was Joseph meant to be powerful, but he had become influential in a very particular time and way so that he could save both Egypt and his own family from famine.

So Joseph tells his brothers, more than 20 years after they'd conspired against him, "You meant evil against me, *but God meant it for good*, to bring it about that many people should be kept alive, as they are today" (Genesis 50:20). The very actions Joseph's brothers took to destroy him were purposed in God's gracious will to bring about salvation—for the family, for the nation, and eventually for the whole world through the Messiah, who would descend from one of Joseph's brothers.

This is the wonder of God's gracious providence: that even the evil we mean to do can be used in his hand to bring about good. So it is the love of God for those I love which anchors me when I'm tossed around by regret and fear—his love and his power to accomplish his perfect will, in spite of my weaknesses. Because, just as my own story and life are more than the natural consequences of my own choices, the lives of those I care for are secure in his hand.

God's gracious providence means he will not allow our imperfections to harm others in ways he cannot redeem. As theologian Sinclair Ferguson has said of Joseph's story, "What a stabilizing thing it is if the devil hammers home at the sin of your past life to see that it was part of the fruit of [Joseph's] brothers' sin … caught up in the providence of God that multitudes were saved from death in these days of famine."[81] Not only does this give us hope when we have failed to love as we should; it also grants us courage to do our imperfect best to love and serve in God's kingdom, because, if God uses what is meant for evil for good, how much more will he be pleased to use our attempts to obey him and love others for good?

It turns out that there were other believers whom God would place in my high-school friend's life. In the conversation we had post-college, she told me that she'd explored Christianity as an undergraduate with Christians who'd explained to her more of the gospel. God's pursuit of her was not bound by my failures and sin. Thank God, it never is.

HIS GRACE IN THE EQUATION

For the perfectionist, life is math. You enter values on one side of an equation, and on the other side, you get what you put in. Which is to say, there is no accounting for grace. But grace is at the heart of Christianity, and the beauty of grace is that it is the antithesis of input determining output. It is the opposite of getting what you deserve.

Our lives are less like equations than they are stories of God's grace. In the best stories, multiple arcs come together in unexpected ways. There is darkness and danger, tragedy and missteps, but in the end, redemption. Such is our story as the people of God. At its center, the darkest act of human sin—the murder of God incarnate—was purposed by God for our salvation. And in the mysterious interaction between our responsibility and God's providence, God has woven many more subplots of grace.

Sometimes, our failures to do as we ought have devastating consequences, and we are not guaranteed that things will return to how they were before. After rashly selling his birthright to his brother Jacob, Esau "sought [the blessing] with tears" but was too late (Hebrews 12:17). Moses, forbidden entrance to the promised land because of his failure to honor God, begged to enter the promised land. God answered, "Enough from you! Never speak to me of this matter again!" (Deuteronomy 3:26). But these consequences weren't the end of their stories. In the grace of God, Esau would come to embrace the brother he had driven out in his murderous rage. Moses would one day stand in Israel with the transfigured Christ (Matthew 17:1-3). And the crucifixion of the Son of God would mean eternal life for many.

"Grace is not a retroactive magic that makes evil good," writes James K.A. Smith in his book, *How to Inhabit Time*. "Easter Sunday's light doesn't obliterate the long, dark shadows of Holy Saturday. Grace doesn't justify evil; grace overcomes it."[82] It is this overcoming nature of grace that assures us that we aren't consigned to a life of trying to minimize the damage we do in this world. Even as we look in horror at the cascade of dominos we've knocked over, someone is at work who is greater than all our sin and guilt. He picks up the pieces we've overturned, redirecting the force of their fall in surprising directions as his grace abounds in our forgiveness and the redemptive purposes of his will.

In light of grace, we even learn to look at our sinful pasts differently. Smith writes:

Shame teaches me to look at my past and see something hideous that makes me regret my existence. In grace, God looks at my past and sees the sketch of a work of art that he wants to finish painting and show the world.[83]

The master Artist is at work in your life, and with grace in the picture, he wastes nothing, not even the choices you are most ashamed of.

In his psalm of repentance for adultery and murder, King David cries out for the Lord to wash and cleanse him. He prays that God would restore him, and, in a line that has always surprised me, declares, "Then I will teach transgressors your ways, and sinners will return to you" (Psalm 51:13). In his wonderful mercy, God not only forgives us but transforms places of shame and guilt into places from which we are able to minister to others, pointing them to the only wellspring of forgiveness and life.

I've seen it in my own story—the way my deepest regrets become places where I encounter the marvelous grace of God. In the moments when I've felt most broken, I have become most convinced of God's grace and have been made to desire more deeply that others know it too. He has turned desert places—the memories of some of my greatest failures—into doorways of hope for others (Hosea 2:15).

Might God be doing the same in you, weaving his story of redemption in your life in such compelling ways that, through your testimony, sinners may turn back to him?

If you have known the taste of tears, kneeling as a sinner at the feet of our beautiful Lord, then you may be one of the people Newton writes about, who, after "long experience of their own deceitful hearts, after repeated proofs of their weakness, willfulness, ingratitude, and insensibility ... find that none of these things can separate them from the love of Jesus."[84] You may wish that your story featured less weakness and failure or needed fewer repeated proofs of his love—but these are the stories we carry. Stories of sinfulness, yes, but also of grace that overcomes. These are the stories that other broken sinners need to hear because, just as his grace has been enough for us, it will be enough for them.

HE GRANTS SLEEP

Our lives are indescribably more than the sum of the good and bad choices we've made up until now. The gracious providence of God lies behind our stories of redemption. It is behind spiritual birth and all growth in his kingdom

(1 Corinthians 3:7). And it is the foundation of soul rest for the weary servant of God.

In Psalm 127:1, the psalmist says that unless the Lord watches over a city, the watchmen watch it in vain. Unless he builds the house, the laborers work in vain. "It is in vain that you rise up early and go late to rest, eating the bread of anxious toil; for he gives to his beloved sleep" (Psalm 127:2). The implication is that because God is working in unseen, powerful ways beyond our own efforts, we can rest. Because he watches over the city and builds the house, we can lay down our plans and tools, leave our posts for the evening, and lie down without fear. We don't need to toil in the anxiety of believing the future is all up to us.

So, we sleep. Like a farmer who wakes, then sows, and then goes to bed, we will rise in the morning to find that seeds have sprouted—though we know not how. This is the mathematics of God's gracious providence—that in the final count, one seed somehow yields thirty-, sixty-, or a hundred-fold. It is the wonder of five loaves and two fish feeding a multitude—the beauty of looking back and seeing that God has fulfilled his purposes for us. Ours is the deep sleep of the beloved who knows that God is building our house and watching over our city and writing our stories in ways more beautiful than we could ask for or imagine—to the praise of his glorious grace.

A PRAYER FOR WHEN YOU FEAR MISSING THE WAY (AND FOR ALL THAT'S LEFT UNDONE)

Sovereign God,

I want to do your will, but the road
before me isn't clear. I want to
choose the path that is best, but
I'm afraid of missing the way.

Maker of heaven and earth, you keep
watch over my coming and going.
Keep me close to you now. Grant me
clarity to see the choices before me with
discerning eyes. Give me godly wisdom
to know the way of faith and love. Fill
me with courage amid uncertainty
and trust in your shepherd's heart.

Whatever you call me to, give me strength
to obey. If you're calling me to walk
without absolute certainty that I've
chosen what is best, remind me of
your gracious providence especially
then. You have led me this far. You are
not going to leave me behind now.

*[You can pray about any specific
decision you need to make here.]*

In all I do, may your will be done.

In all that is left undone, may
your grace be sufficient.

Most of all, I entrust to you those who will
be affected by my actions. When I fear my
failures and inadequacies will bring them
harm, remind me of your grace and power
to accomplish your good purposes in their
lives in spite of and even through me.

You love these dear ones more than I do.
By this, my heart is comforted, and
In your love for both them and me,
I rest.

In Jesus' name,
Amen

Scripture reference: Psalm 121:7-8

CHAPTER 8

LOVE

*To please God ... to be a real ingredient in the divine
happiness ... to be loved by God, not merely pitied, but
delighted in as an artist delights in his work or a father
in a son—it seems impossible, a weight or burden of glory
which our thoughts can hardly sustain. But so it is.*

C.S. LEWIS

I am living proof that Christianity and doubt aren't
incompatible. Over the years, I've experienced doubt
like a carpet pulled out from beneath my feet. I've felt it
like an almost imperceptible but persistent tapping on the
shoulder. I've faced it in outright temptations to accuse God
of wrongdoing. I've also known it as a fog.

The fog descended during that season of God's wounding
as my sin was spotlighted. My doubt was amorphous but
ever present. It filled the air like smoke, but I struggled to
find its source.

This time, I knew I wasn't doubting whether God really
made the world or if the Bible was true. I'd accepted the
exclusive claims of Christ for salvation and was convinced
of his deep love for the people I served. So what exactly was
I doubting?

The answer came as I stood in front of the mirror, having
failed again. Sinned again. Filled with disgust and self-loathing,

the words came out as the most forthright prayer I'd ever prayed up to that point: "God, I don't believe you love me."

I KNOW GOD LOVES ME, BUT

There are many reasons why Christians may struggle to feel God's love. Christian perfectionists may be quick to assume that the reason is sin, but that isn't always the case. Sometimes physical or mental illness, past trauma, intense suffering, or burnout affects our bodies and minds so that it's hard to sense the love of God. Some of us struggle because of the way in which God has been represented in our religious experiences and churches. More often than not, there isn't one reason we can pinpoint. We just know we have trouble feeling that God truly loves us given our imperfections.

"Jesus loves me, this I know" goes the classic children's chorus—but there's knowing, and there's *knowing*. There's acknowledging God's love as a truth statement, and there's believing, experiencing, and delighting in this love. "I know that God loves me," a Christian perfectionist may say, "but I don't *feel* it." "I know God loves me, but I feel like he's unhappy with me." "I know he loves me, but I'm not sure how much I really believe it."

Maybe you've experienced God's love in the past, but as you've wrestled with indwelling sin, shame has displaced any sense of his delight. Or perhaps his love has always felt more like an abstract truth than a lived reality. Maybe, as you pursue holiness, it has felt safer to see God as demanding and displeased than accepting, warm, and kind. You don't want to be irreverent or presumptuous.

But it is not presumptuous to see God as loving and kind. God's love has always been a source of great joy for his people, not just as a one-time life-changing event but in daily experience. In the Old Testament, Moses taught God's people to sing, "Satisfy us in the morning with your steadfast love, that we may rejoice and be glad all our days" (Psalm 90:14). In the New Testament, we are told to abide in this love (John 15:9).

As sure as God is holy, he is love (1 John 4:8). And as much as he wants us to know him in his perfect righteousness, he wants us to know him in his perfect love.

Here is where our hearts push back:

I know God is loving, but could he really love me?

I know God loves me, but that doesn't mean he's happy with me.

I know God loves this other person who's holier, humbler, and kinder than I am, but I'm—well, I'm me.

Yes, Jesus loves me, but how do I truly know?

The children's chorus answers that last question with "The Bible tells me so." Taking that as our cue, we turn there now.

GOD'S LOVE FOR SINNERS

The heart of my prayer as I stood full of doubt in front of the mirror was whether the all-knowing, holy God would love a sinner like me. Did he *really* love me? Could he truly treasure and feel affection for one who's been forgiven and *still* continues to fall? The answer given in the Bible is a resounding, "Yes!"

In Exodus, God proclaims that he is...

the LORD, the LORD, a God merciful and gracious, slow to anger, and abounding in steadfast love and faithfulness,

keeping steadfast love for thousands, forgiving iniquity
and transgression and sin, but who will by no means
clear the guilty, visiting the iniquity of the fathers on the
children and the children's children, to the third and the
fourth generation. (Exodus 34:6-7)

This is God according to himself. He shows favor to the undeserving. He doesn't easily get angry. He forgives transgressions. All these are descriptions of God's love *for sinners*. Those who are perfect do not need mercy. It's sinners who need grace, patience, and forgiveness—sinners who are recipients of his steadfast love. Yes, God doesn't just "clear the guilty" (remember, he justifies sinners through Christ, not by ignoring sin), but even so, the consequences of their sins last a few generations in contrast to the promise of his love to *thousands* of generations.

These are not empty words. God's declaration of his steadfast love in Exodus comes after his people have done great evil. Just a few chapters after promising their full obedience to God, the Israelites made a golden calf, worshiping it and crediting it for their deliverance from Egypt (Exodus 24:3; 32:4). Instead of destroying this ungrateful, idolatrous, and rebellious people, God shows mercy and spares them. Then, he pledges to lead and love them still.

LOVE MADE MANIFEST

Through the rest of the Old Testament, God's description of himself as gracious and merciful, slow to anger, and abounding in steadfast love is repeated to those who keep flip-flopping between worship and idolatry (Numbers 14:18; Nehemiah 9:17; Psalm 86:15; Joel 2:13; Jonah 4:2). His love is tested and proved time and time again, all the way up to the

New Testament, where his love is fully "made manifest among us" in the coming of Christ (1 John 4:9).

If you have any doubt as to whether God loves sinners, read the Gospels and study Jesus. There, you'll meet God in flesh who keeps company with rebels and eats with the spiritually sick (Mark 2:15-17). See how he does not condemn a woman exposed in her greatest shame but rescues and calls her to a new life (John 8:1-11). How he looks with love on a young man who loves money more than God (Mark 10:17-22). Even at the height of his suffering, at the brink of death, he holds no contempt for his torturers, praying instead for their forgiveness (Luke 23:34). There, in his death on a cross, God's love was put on supreme, glorious display for all to see.

Jesus died because God loves sinners. I know this may sound basic, but I think sometimes we skirt around it or explain it away. I read an article once by a pastor describing how Christians sometimes approach God's love almost like money launderers, trying to keep the source of their money hidden by layering financial accounts:

> *This is what I do. I layer it. Instead of just letting it explode on my lap like a theological firecracker, I say, "It's for His glory that he elected me despite my deadness in sin, and on and on..." True though all of that may be, it is not supposed to cut the wires of divine love.*[85]

Whether out of familiarity or fear of misrepresenting God's holiness or just because his love is so intense, Christians can inadvertently "layer" God's display of love on the cross. Perhaps you acknowledge Jesus' death as something he did in obedience to the Father. Maybe you recognize it as an act of great sacrifice to bring about God's glory. But if you do not receive the cross of Christ as a demonstration of God's incredible love for you just as you are, even in your sin, then you'll miss knowing his mercy and grace for you, and the glory and wonder of his love.

Scripture abounds with instances of the incredible claim that Jesus died on the cross because of God's love, and specifically because of God's love for sinners. "God *shows his love* for us in that *while we were still sinners*, Christ died for us" (Romans 5:8). "*Because of his great love for us,* God, who is rich in mercy, made us alive with Christ *even when we were dead in transgressions*" (Ephesians 2:4-5, NIV). It's because "God so loved the world" that he gave his Son (John 3:16). And for the very same love, the Son willingly laid down his life (John 15:13, 1 John 3:16).

What's more, God's love is personal. God did not just love "the world" as an amorphous crowd of nameless sinners; he "loved *me* and gave himself for *me*" (Galatians 2:20). His saving love is set on you and me as individuals, and he proved it in his life and death.

This was God's answer to me in my doubt. As soon as I raised my challenge against heaven—*I don't believe you love me*—an image of the cross came to mind, and I understood and wept. Yes, I was a great sinner. But the cross was proof that he loved me *even while I was in my sin*. And rather than strike me down for questioning his great act of love, he instead spoke gently to acknowledge and address my struggle: *You don't believe that I love you? Here's how I showed it.*

HE LOVES YOU BECAUSE HE LOVES YOU

Why though? *Why do you love me?* romantic partners want to know from one another. *Why do you put up with me?* we ask friends who stick with us in our ugliest times. There's something about unmerited love—love that persists in spite of our not deserving it—that throws our minds for a loop. I think this is one of the impulses behind our "money laundering" of God's love. Perhaps if we can explain it, we'll be able to accept it, because, although it might make sense for someone to die for a good person, why would God love me, messed up and broken as I am?

God answers this question—kind of. In Deuteronomy, Moses speaks to the Israelites at the tail end of their journey through the wilderness. He sets up the question of why, saying:

> *The LORD your God has chosen you to be a people for*
> *his treasured possession, out of all the peoples who are*
> *on the face of the earth. It was not because you were*
> *more in number than any other people that the LORD*
> *set his love on you and chose you, for you were the fewest*
> *of all peoples, but it is because the LORD loves you and*
> *is keeping the oath that he swore to your fathers, that*
> *the LORD has brought you out with a mighty hand and*
> *redeemed you from the house of slavery, from the hand of*
> *Pharaoh king of Egypt. (Deuteronomy 7:6b-8)*

Why did God choose his people to be his treasured possession? Why did he set his love on them? Not because of their greatness but *"because the LORD loves you"* and because he was keeping his promises—promises he had made to their ancestors because he'd "set his affection on" them and loved them too (Deuteronomy 10:15). Similar language is used in the New Testament when the apostle Paul writes that "in love, [God] predestined us for adoption to himself ... according to the purpose of his will" (Ephesians 1:4-5). In these passages, the answer behind God's choice to love is simply that—God's choice and God's love.

In this way, God's love is different than how we usually experience love in the world. We understand love as affection kindled and sustained because of something in the beloved—"I love you because of how you love me" or "I love you because you're beautiful and special." "I love you because of how I feel when I'm with you," and even "I love you because you're mine."

There's nothing wrong with love that is awakened because of something lovely in another person. That kind of love is natural and beautiful, and a gift. But God's love is not like that. There is no explanation for God's love outside of itself because his love for us originates from within himself. As one theologian put it, "Nothing lies in back of this love."[86] The more we try to peek behind the curtain to find the "real" reason why he loves us, the more we will see that the reason is simply God and his love.

God loves us because he loves us. As much as this may feel like a non-answer, it is the answer we need. There is freedom and rest to be found in being loved with a love we did not earn because it is a love that we cannot lose. Before you could love God or do anything for him—before you even existed—God loved you with an everlasting love. Nothing you do can make him love you more. Nothing you do will make him love you less.

The unshakable nature of this love is expressed beautifully in Paul's letter to the Romans:

For I am sure that neither death nor life, nor angels
nor rulers, nor things present nor things to come, nor
powers, nor height nor depth, nor anything else in all

creation, will be able to separate us from the love of God in Christ Jesus our Lord. (Romans 8:38-39)

You are lavishly loved with a love that predates the foundations of the world. Nothing, believer—not your past regrets, not your present weakness, not your future sin—nothing in all creation, yourself included, will ever separate you from this love. God's love is his to freely give, and he has chosen to set his affections upon you.

HE DELIGHTS IN YOU

"I know God loves me," the Christian perfectionist might say. "I just feel like he's never happy with me."

I've observed this sentiment in Asian-American immigrant communities, where parental love is often expressed through sacrifice rather than in verbal affirmation. To ask whether our parents love us borders the offensive. Many of them left behind status, security, and home for the sake of their children's futures. If they hold us to high standards, it's because they want the best for us. Of course they love us. But to ask whether our parents are happy with us—that is a different question. In the same way, you can be convinced of God's sacrificial love while failing to perceive his delight.

As Christians, one of our greatest motivations for obedience is seeking God's pleasure (1 Thessalonians 2:4; 4:1). It is good and appropriate for children to want to please their parents and seek their approval. But whether or not we feel that it is possible to please our Father will determine the way we approach the Christian life. If it seems that our attempts at obedience are never good enough, we'll constantly be on edge or ready to give up, anxious about messing up or reticent to try again when we fail. But what if God is delighted with our wobbly steps of obedience, faltering though they may be?

In his book *The Hole in our Holiness*, pastor Kevin DeYoung writes about God's pleasure in our heartfelt attempts at obedience:

> *Our God is not a capricious slave driver. He is not hypersensitive and prone to fits of rage on account of slight offenses. He is slow to anger and abounding in steadfast love (Exodus 34:6). "He is not hard to please," Tozer reminds us, "though he may be hard to satisfy."*
>
> *Why do we imagine God to be so unmoved by our heartfelt attempts at obedience? He is, after all, our Heavenly Father. What sort of father looks at his daughter's homemade birthday card and complains that the color scheme is all wrong? What kind of mother says to her son, after he gladly cleaned the garage but put the paint cans on the wrong shelf, "This is worthless in my sight"? ... Many of our righteous deeds are not only not filthy in God's eyes, they are exceedingly sweet, precious, and pleasing to him.*[87]

Perhaps you feel that because of your imperfections, God must look at your efforts to please him with disappointment, anger, or apathy. Maybe you compare your spirituality to others who seem closer to God, holier or more loving than you are, and you conclude that he'd never be happy with what you have to offer. This couldn't be further from the truth.

Just as a parent looks at their child's gift and joyfully receives it because they know the effort their child put into it, God is your compassionate Father, who knows your frame (Psalm 103:13-14). He does not wait until you are perfect before accepting your gifts, nor is he comparing you with his other children. Though you may wish you could offer *purer* motives, *more* wholeheartedness, and *greater* selflessness, he is pleased with your heart's desire to obey him. "She has done what she could," were Jesus' words of affirmation as he lovingly accepted a woman and her offering (Mark 14:8). Ever the gracious receiver, he looks at your willingness and not at what you're unable to give (2 Corinthians 8:12).

My three-year-old recently drew a picture for her dad. She filled the paper with pencil-shaded hearts. With marker, she added purple smiley faces, and colored circles of blue, orange, yellow, and green. I watched her work diligently on it and then suddenly crumple it in frustration. She'd scribbled on it, she told me, and when I smoothed it out and encouraged her to give it to her dad anyway, her eyes filled with tears as she said, "He's not going to like it." But I know he would have loved it.

Your heavenly Father will not reject your heartfelt attempts at obedience, even if you've accidentally scribbled. He is not hard to please but is delighted in you as you seek to walk in his ways (Proverbs 11:20). He takes pleasure in you as you worship him and hope in his love (Psalm 147:11). You are his child, and whether you come to him with two coins or a treasure worth a year's wages or a scrunched up-drawing of purple smileys, he receives you and your gift with joy (Mark 12:41-44; John 12:1-8).

EARTHLY LOVES
Maybe you don't have trouble believing God loves you, but it still feels more like a distant truth than present experience. One of the limitations of dealing with Christian perfectionism in a book is that, more often than not, God chooses to show

us his love and leads us to his rest through other people, especially the people of God.

God's love can be hard to feel because we can't see him. In his first letter, the apostle John acknowledges this, saying, "No one has ever seen God." However, he continues, "If we love one another, God abides in us and his love is perfected in us" (1 John 4:12). God's love shines through the prism of our earthly relationships, and as we trace the beams up to their source, we begin to recognize the warmth and brilliance of divine affection.

I think of this sometimes when I am floored by the love of another. *What if I believed that God loved me as much as this person does?* I would be so much more eager to approach God, to talk to him, and to receive his affection for me, if I believed his love for me matched the love and delight of those who love me the most in this world.

The incredible truth is that the love of those who love me is a gift from Love himself. His love for me is matchless, extending as high as the heavens are above the earth (Psalm 103:11). The kindness and care of others is tangible evidence of his infinite kindness and grace: a healing drop from the life-giving well of his steadfast love.

Can you think of anyone in your life who has loved you well? Anyone who has been patient, kind, slow to anger, and persevering with you? Anyone who has hoped for you? Who has seen your weaknesses and still loved you? From whom you've asked for forgiveness and received it freely?

Perhaps it's that friend who asks, "How are you?" and listens with compassion. Or the parent who is always ready to welcome you home, glad to spend time with you. Maybe it's the spiritual mentor who has walked with you through doubt, fear, and failure. What difference would it make for you to receive their love for you as evidence of God's love, like someone bringing back a small gift from a far-off land? What difference would it make to think that, as incredibly healing and wonderful as their love is, it is but a sample of the expansive storehouse of love God has for you?

Maybe considering other people's love is just as hard for you as thinking of God's love because you feel unworthy of their care. If so, perhaps it would be helpful to think of those you love instead. Think of your joy at your sister's, brother's, or child's flourishing. Think of the ways you delight in a dear friend. Think of someone you have felt compassion and concern for lately. Can you imagine yourself being similarly loved, and much, much more? As Sibbes writes, "Shall there be more mercy in the stream than in the spring? Shall we think there is more mercy in ourselves than in God, who plants the affection of mercy in us?"[88] You love these dear ones so much. Your love is a taste of the boundless love of God not just for them but for you.

LOVE BEYOND COMPREHENSION

If you are still feeling that you need help to truly know God's love, it's because you do—we all do. Just as we rely on God's power for spiritual growth, we need divine enabling to grow in knowledge of God's love. We need the Spirit's strength. We also need a supernatural faith.

Years ago, I took a cruise through Alaska. The cleanness of the air, the clarity of the sky, the enormity of age-old glaciers—it all felt realer than real. I'd never been so immersed in beauty at every angle and depth of view. From the floes on the water to near cliffs to the distant mountains, I tried to soak in every bit of it but discovered I could only process as much as my senses allowed, one moment at a time.

God's love is like the most magnificent of views. We can wake up to receive it anew, intentionally explore more of its corners and depths, and learn to better describe its beauty in each season, but it will never be manageable and fully comprehended. In fact, his love is so great that it "surpasses knowledge," writes the apostle Paul (Ephesians 3:19). So he prays that God's people would have "strength to comprehend with all the saints" the breadth, length, height, and depth of Christ's love (v 18-19).

God's love is so great that we need the Spirit's power to comprehend it. We also need faith. 1 John 4:16 says, "We have come to know and to *believe* the love that God has for us." We need faith because it doesn't make sense that God would delight in people who continually fail him. It doesn't make sense that the Creator of the universe would take pleasure in our imperfect obedience. It doesn't make sense that God would die for sinners—and in some ways it isn't supposed to.

Perhaps that's the reason why Jesus says those who have been forgiven much will love much (Luke 7:47). Because only when we know our own fallenness do we begin to feel the incomprehensible nature of God's love. Others may take his love as a given. ("Of course God loves me; what's not to love?") You who know your sin, failures, and weaknesses— everything that makes God's love seem too good to be true— need to receive it by *faith*. But in believing, you will come to know a love that is beyond reason. A love that surpasses knowledge. A love that doesn't make sense by any human standards but is nonetheless marvelously, wonderfully beyond your wildest dreams true.

LOVE (III)

In his poem *Love (III)*, the 17th-century minister George Herbert writes as one invited to a feast laid out by God. There's this constant back and forth in the poem between him and God ("Love"). Herbert's protestations—he's too sinful, he has nothing to give, he's unworthy—are patiently attended to by Love, who calls him near.

In this chapter I've tried to address a few questions we may have about God's love, but I know from experience that we can be quite nimble when it comes to the love of God. Our questions multiply as we try to slip away from God's kind and steady gaze. Still, there comes a point when, having been invited to his table and shown the feast, having had the food explained to us and our objections of our unworthiness addressed, the next step for us is to taste it in faith.

So it is with Herbert in his poem. Beloved, if you hear the invitation of Love today, I pray you'd also sit and eat.

Love bade me welcome. Yet my soul drew back
    Guilty of dust and sin.
But quick-eyed Love, observing me grow slack
    From my first entrance in,
Drew nearer to me, sweetly questioning,
    If I lacked any thing.

A guest, I answered, worthy to be here:
    Love said, You shall be he.
I the unkind, ungrateful? Ah my dear,
    I cannot look on thee.
Love took my hand, and smiling did reply,
    Who made the eyes but I?

Truth Lord, but I have marred them: let my shame
    Go where it doth deserve.
And know you not, says Love, who bore the blame?
    My dear, then I will serve.
You must sit down, says Love, and taste my meat:
    So I did sit and eat.

             "Love (III)", George Herbert[89]

A PRAYER FOR WHEN YOUR BEST DOESN'T FEEL GOOD ENOUGH

Gracious God,

My soul blesses your name. Thank you
for forgiving all my sins and healing
me, for redeeming my life from the
pit and crowning me with love and
compassion. You satisfy my desires
with good things and renew me day
by day. From every possible view of
my life, I see grace upon grace.

Lord, you have been so good to me that
I wish I had an offering worthy of you.
Yet when I consider what I have, none
of it seems enough. Still, in view of your
mercy, I am compelled to bring what I
have—to offer myself as a living sacrifice.

I offer you my worship.
Fill my days with thanksgiving and
my mouth with your praise.

I offer my strength in service to your kingdom.
In my workplace, at home, at church,
in my community, and in the world,
help me love others with all that I
am and have. Increase my love that
it may abound more and more.

I offer you my weaknesses.
  In my insufficiencies, may your
  grace and strength be made
  perfect and put on display.

I offer you… *[Here you can pray
  about any specific gifts, weaknesses,
  etc. that God brings to mind.]*

God, I don't have much, but everything
  I have, I give to you. Thank you for
  stooping down to receive me and my
  gifts so graciously. Though my heart
  feels the smallness of my offering, I
  offer even that to you too—the sadness
  that I don't have more to give.

My broken and contrite heart,
  O God, you will not despise.
Be pleased to make it yours.

In Jesus' name,
Amen

---

*Scripture references: Psalm 103:1-5; Romans 12:1; 2 Corinthians 12:9;
Psalm 51:16-17*

CHAPTER 9

THERE REMAINS A REST

*The final secret, I think, is this, that the words
"You shall love the Lord your God" become in
the end less a command than a promise. And the
promise is that, yes, on the weary feet of faith and
the fragile wings of hope, we will come to love
him at last as from the first he has loved us.*

FREDERICK BUECHNER

There are still weeks when my conscience is loud. Here is a recent example: I'm preparing mid-week to lead worship on Sunday. I've been angry and irritable, and the Holy Spirit is showing me the ways in which I rely on myself in parenting. I need so much help, yet I pray so little. Just yesterday, I yelled at one of my kids, and regret lingers.

Preparing the worship set, I am anxious about picking the right songs. I feel a niggling tug toward self-focus—the dreadful impulse to make even God's worship about my glory: how *I* sound, how well *I* lead. I hear the rattling of accusatory thoughts coming down the pipeline, ready to cast suspicion on my motives. I am also keenly aware of the limits of my service. Only God can draw true praise out of the hearts of his people.

Growth in faith for me looks like pressing on through the noise. Where, in the past, I would have frozen as if at a dead end, I now practice pulling up to this busy intersection, observing the stop sign and driving on as soon as it's safe. The sins I have undoubtedly committed, I confess. But I do not take the bait on introspection and fear. ("Do it to serve," my husband often reminds me when I'm getting sucked into the black hole of *What if I'm doing all of this for the wrong reasons without knowing it even though I don't want to?*)

So, by the grace of God, I choose worship and service. I choose the set, trusting in God's providence. I ask the team to pray for me, and we ask God to do what only he can do in our church. We practice, and on the Lord's Day, I stand and sing salvation songs with the people of God.

In faith, we sing of Jesus' finished work and of the welcome of God. We rejoice that sin's curse is broken and that we are freed from fear and darkness. In freedom, we live and we love. "Onward!" we cry out, to eternal glory and to God![90]

This is the Sabbath, when Christian perfectionists like me, wrestling with sin, condemnation, and loud consciences, are invited to find rest for our souls. Here, footworn sinner-saints catch their breath. Together, we are strengthened on the journey to the great and final Sabbath to come.

SABBATH REST

Having answered Jesus' call for the heavy-laden to come to him, the Christian perfectionist may wonder, "Why do I still feel so tired?" If God has promised rest for my soul, why don't I feel a sense of restfulness all the time (and does this mean I'm doing something wrong)?

We started this book by considering the ways in which Christian perfectionism is an ache for what was lost in Eden. But our desire for perfection is not just for what *was* or even what *could have been*—it is a longing for a future that God has told us *will be*. And one reason why we will feel weary and burdened, even after coming to Jesus, is that we are still waiting for a rest and perfection that is to come.

One way in which the Bible describes our promised future is as "Sabbath rest." When we hear "Sabbath," we may immediately think of prohibitions—maybe the Old Testament command to cease from work once a week or advice we've heard about establishing a regular rhythm of not checking our phones and emails. But the Bible's definition of Sabbath (and of rest) conveys more than "not working." Similar to the biblical ideas of peace and perfection, it encompasses the idea of consummation—of fullness, glory, and celebration at the close of good work.

In the Old Testament, the weekly Sabbath mirrored the pattern of work and rest that God set at creation. God created the world in six days and rested on the seventh (Exodus 20:11). His rest was not recuperation (God doesn't get tired) or inactivity (God didn't stop upholding creation). Rather, it signified completion, joy, and satisfaction in his work.[91]

God's rest on the seventh day was like the rest of an artist who sits down to enjoy his masterpiece after putting on final touches, or an athlete who finishes her course and receives a medal. This kind of rest was what the apostle Paul looked forward to at the end of his life when he said, "I have fought the good fight, I have finished the race, I have kept the faith. Henceforth there is laid up for me the crown of righteousness, which the Lord, the righteous judge, will award to me on that day, and not only to me but also to all who have loved his appearing" (2 Timothy 4:7-8). It is the rest of the servant whose Master has said, *Well done, good and faithful servant. Enter into my joy* (Matthew 25:23). And it is the rest that awaits us after our work on earth is done.

The New Testament writer of Hebrews explains that by faith, we have access to the same rest that God entered after creation. Through Christ, we enter God's "Sabbath rest" (Hebrews 4:3, 9-10). This rest is both present and future—both individual and cosmic in scope. In this life, we know it in part, but when Christ returns, all of creation will know it in full.

The future aspect of Sabbath rest helps us make sense of our tiredness. I have written this book with the conviction that God gives us rest in this life, and I pray that you will experience God's rest in increasing measure. But the work God calls you to—your perseverance in the faith, your fight against sin, your acts of love—will be exhausting at times. Serving God and his people, even from a place of peace, you may find yourself burdened beyond what you feel you can bear (2 Corinthians 1:8). In a fallen world full of thorns, even good work can be heart- and back-breaking.

If you are sensing the weight of Jesus' yoke and burden, you aren't doing something wrong. You feel this weight because, just as God worked for six days, you also work for now. But there is a rest for your soul that is coming. The seventh day draws near.

On that day, God will "wipe away every tear from [our] eyes, and death shall be no more, neither shall there be mourning, nor crying, nor pain anymore, for the former things have passed away" (Revelation 21:4). When Jesus returns, he will establish a new heaven and new earth (v 1). He will reign in righteousness and peace, and all creation will know his rest.

In his presence, your worship will be unhindered and your peace unbreakable. You will not doubt his delight in you when you hear his voice declare before angels and all people that you belong to him. The voice of Satan, the tempter and accuser, will be silenced once and for all (20:7-10). There will be no more testing to endure—for Christ has conquered, and you will reign with him (22:5).

This promise of a final Sabbath rest casts a new light on our present struggles. The 5th-century bishop Augustine once described the whole life of a Christian as a stretching of desire. Just as we might stretch the opening of a bag to make room for what it's going to hold, "God, by deferring our hope, stretches our desire" so that we will be ready to receive what is coming.[92] If the world that is to come is truly as good as God says it will be, then our longings for rest and peace, righteousness and flourishing, perfection and communion with God are holy desires preparing us for Jesus' return. They are tutors, teaching us to "[love] his appearing" as we look to the day when our labors give way to everlasting rest and we enter into our Master's joy (2 Timothy 4:8; Revelation 14:13).

The Lord of heaven and earth is making all things new (21:5). As you wait for the Sabbath to come, you will need this hope cemented in your heart.

GLORY

Up until now, we've mainly considered how we can rest from perfectionistic concerns—negative evaluations, guilt, anxiety, and fears that plague our pursuit of Christ. We've done this acknowledging that we are called to strive for the perfection God commands. But one day, we won't need to strive. You and I are heading for glory, and this glory is, in the words of author Nancy Guthrie, "even better than Eden."[93]

C.S. Lewis's novel *Perelandra* conveys this idea through a parallel history on another planet. In the story, the main character, Ransom, is sent from earth to Perelandra (Venus). Perelandra is a perfect paradise, a pre-fall Eden, and just as in Eden, the devil tempts the queen to disobey the law of God ("Maleldil"). Through great trial, Ransom destroys the devil, and the queen does not rebel against Maleldil's word. Thus, the course of Perelandran history is set. Not only are the king and queen spared a great fall; they step into a new beginning. As a messenger of Maleldil tells Ransom after the queen's testing:

> *The world is born today ... Today for the first time two creatures of the low worlds, two images of Maleldil that breathe and breed like the beasts, step up that step at which your parents fell, and sit in the throne of what they were meant to be.*[94]

From the beginning, humanity was meant for a greater glory than that which we had in Eden. Though Adam and Eve were sinless, their position was not yet secure—they could still fall. But their decision regarding the tree of the knowledge of good and evil was a historical inflection point. They could obey and, in God's time, receive eternal life—a perfect future in which humanity would never be tempted again.[95] Or they could disobey and bring death to all. As Lewis writes, from there they would "go up or go down, into corruption or into perfection."[96]

In attempting to obtain glory apart from God, Adam chose death and corruption for all. But the good news of the gospel is that we have a "second Adam," whose obedience leads us into life and perfection.

When he walked this earth, Jesus lived in perfect submission to the Father. After dying for our sins, he rose from the grave and, in doing so, did much more than restore us to Eden.

Raised to an imperishable body, Jesus was the first person to "step up that step" where Adam and Eve had fallen. He was resurrected to a glorified body, and one day, those who trust him will also rise (1 Corinthians 15:20-23).

This is our certain hope on our worst and best of days, on days when it feels like we are broken beyond mending and on days when we are certain God really *is* doing something beautiful in us: that as surely as Christ rose from the grave, so will we. Though for now, we painfully and slowly plod along in our sanctification, when Jesus comes back, we will be changed in the twinkling of an eye (v 51-52). In an instant, we will be glorified: fully transformed into his image and given resurrected bodies like his, which the curse of sin will never touch again (Romans 8:30; 1 Corinthians 15:42-49). Death will be swallowed up in victory and we will put on immortality (v 53-55).

So we find that the life the Christian perfectionist longs for—where there are no wrong paths, where every decision only leads to greater flourishing, and where everything we could ever desire is good, a life of everlasting rest and unbreakable communion with God—is the life we are destined for. We were made for glory. It was always God's gracious intention to grant it, and he has restored it to us in Christ.

When Jesus comes back, we will become who we've always been meant to be. Following in the footsteps of our risen Lord, we will step up that step where Adam and Eve fell. And from there, we will never fall again.

YOU ARE NOT YET WHAT YOU WILL BE
This vision of our future selves may seem remote, but it's precisely when it feels far away that we need it the most.

Remembering it is like reviewing the 3D schematics for a house renovation while in the middle of demolition. It's a reminder of what is coming and what all the stress is for: proof that piles of broken drywall won't be sitting in the hallway forever.

The apostle John writes about the importance of remembering our glorification and Christ's return. His first epistle is addressed to believers who are clearly in process. In the letter, there's this constant back-and-forth between commands to righteousness ("I am writing these things to you so that you may not sin") and strong assurances of forgiveness ("But if anyone does sin, we have an advocate") (1 John 2:1). It's in this context that John tells of a coming day when we will no longer be in-process:

Beloved, we are God's children now, and what we will be has not yet appeared; but we know that when he appears we shall be like him, because we shall see him as he is. And everyone who thus hopes in him purifies himself as he is pure. (1 John 3:2-3)

Sometimes, the seemingly unending nature of our fight against sin fuels discouragement. We look at the exposed pipes and wiring, the overwhelming amount of work this fixer-upper is going to take before it's livable, and we're convinced by what we see that we'll be in this state indefinitely. But John reminds us of two things.

First, he says, you are beloved children of God *now* (v 2). Even now, when you are unfinished, God loves you and calls you his own. He loves you with full knowledge that you aren't yet who you will be. And that's the second thing—you aren't yet *who you will be.*

Though you may wrestle for now with the remaining vestiges of your sinful nature, one day you will have faced your last temptation. You will have struggled to do what's right, failed, grieved, and repented for the last time. Then, waking to glory, you will find that you finally love God with all your heart, soul, mind, and strength. Every desire you have will be holy and pure, good and beautiful, excellent and praiseworthy. The weariness of persevering through trial and fighting for faith will be shed like an old coat, and you will be clothed in strength and immortality. You will see him. And seeing him, you will be made like him.

When you feel disheartened by all that you are *not yet*, remember who you *will be*. Though your sin and weakness may seem to overshadow the good work God is doing in you, his Spirit-wrought change in your life is permanent. Your sinfulness will come to an end. But the fruit of his holy work in you? The great and small victories over sin, the steps of courage and faith, the acts of love and good works? Those beautiful evidences of God's grace will be true of you forever.

Beloved child of God, his work in you thus far is the slow lightening of the sky above the horizon as the stars fade.[97] Night is still passing, but take heart. An unending day is coming, and the brightness of that day will be glorious.

I CAN DO IT WITH HELP

One temptation for those of us who have struggled with Christian perfectionism for a long time is to shrink back from pursuing God. Exhausted from our fearful striving and believing God to be perpetually upset with us, we begin to lie low. Afraid of the obedience he might demand, we stop asking him to speak to us. We may even stop repenting, afraid to risk trying only to fail again.

Maybe this is where you find yourself right now. If following Jesus seems impossibly hard, know that you are not expected to take up his yoke and burden on your own. Your gentle and lowly Savior has promised to teach you, and the same power that brought him up from the grave and seated him in the heavenly places is changing you from the inside out (Ephesians 1:19-21).

One of the mysterious realities of the Christian life is that God not only works on but *in* us. He "works in us that which is pleasing to him," such that both the desire and ability to do his will come from him (Hebrews 13:21; Philippians 2:12-13). For Christians, this isn't just a theological idea; it's a lived reality. I have known this reality in the way God has answered prayers to *help me want to want to do his will*. Paul knew it to the point where he could say he toiled with "all [God's] energy that he powerfully works within me" (Colossians 1:29). "I worked harder than any of them," he wrote elsewhere, "though it was not I, but the grace of God that is with me" (1 Corinthians 15:10).

My husband has often said that one thing he enjoys about preaching is that it keeps him mindful of "the gap." As a pastor, he is constantly in a position where the outcomes he desires (people knowing and loving God) are beyond his power to bring about. He can preach, but only God can change hearts. This gap, he says, is an opportunity for dependence. As believers waiting for Christ's return, we will be aware (often painfully so) of the discrepancy between who we are and who we ought to be. One day, God will close this gap completely, but through the Holy Spirit, we experience God in that gap even now.

The Holy Spirit is a guarantee—a kind of down-payment of our resurrection that God gives believers (2 Corinthians 1:22; Romans 8:11). Because he dwells in us, we get a sample of our future glory. This means that though the Spirit's work in you is not yet complete, it has already begun. Even now, you experience his life and peace. He is changing your desires. He produces the fruit of love and joy in you. More powerful than sin, death, and Satan, he gives you supernatural power to obey, change, repent, and persevere.

Years ago, one of my kids went through a phase where her knee-jerk reaction to being asked to do something that seemed hard was "But I caaaan't!" One way we got her out of that habit was teaching her to say instead, "I can do it with help." Is there a hard obedience that God seems to be requiring of you? Maybe it's that growth in purity, holiness, or love that you have been too afraid to ask him for because you're scared to try again. Or that step of faith you know is beyond your own strength to take. You may be weak, but the one who lives in you is strong, and he is able.

Of God's ability to do the impossible, Newton writes:

> *Hope then, my soul, against hope; though your graces are faint and languid, he who planted them will water his own work, and not allow them wholly to die. He can make a little one as a thousand; at his presence mountains sink into plains, streams gush out of the flinty rock, and the wilderness blossoms as the rose. He can pull down what sin builds up, and build up what sin pulls down; that which was impossible to us, is easy to him.*[98]

God is able bring about the change he seeks in you. So it is that Augustine repeatedly and famously prayed, "Grant what you command, and command what you wish."[99] With courage you can say, "God, ask of me what you will," because in the same breath you can also plead, "Holy Spirit, help me to obey."

HE WILL CARRY YOU

He who began a good work in you will be faithful to bring it to completion on the day of Christ's return (Philippians 1:6). But maybe that seems too far in the future for you. Perhaps you feel keenly the wavering of your heart. You do not trust your commitment to follow Christ. Your faith is a flickering flame, and though the air is still for now, a stray wind would blow it out. With the finish line in the distance and so many opportunities to fall between here and there, "How will I ever make it?"

I want to close us here with my favorite benediction in Scripture. It comes at the end of Jude, a tiny book holding this massive ballast of a promise:

Now to him who is able to keep you from stumbling and to present you blameless before the presence of his glory with great joy, to the only God, our Savior, through Jesus Christ our Lord, be glory, majesty, dominion, and authority, before all time and now and forever. Amen.

(Jude v 24-25)

The God of all majesty, your King, uses his power to keep you. Sin does not and will not have dominion over you because dominion and authority belong to him—and so do you (Romans 6:14-18). He will present you blameless before his presence with great joy one day. And he will keep you until that day.

"You have seen how the LORD your God carried you," Moses said to the Israelites at the end of their 40-year journey through the wilderness. The whole way from Egypt to the promised land, "the LORD your God carried you as a man carries his son, all the way that you went until you came to this place" (Deuteronomy 1:31).

I am reminded here of one of the most moving moments in Olympic history. In 1992, sprinter Derek Redmond was looking to medal in the 400-meters when, in the middle of the semifinals, his hamstring tore. In the video of the race, you see him clutch the back of his leg mid-run and kneel on the track. As the other racers finish, he gets back up. Determined to continue, he half-jogs, half-hops down his lane in incredible pain. Suddenly, a man appears, pushing past security and running up to Derek. It's his father.

Jogging alongside his injured son, Jim Redmond puts an arm around Derek's waist. After a few more yards of hopping, Derek slows his pace, throws his arm around his father's neck, and cries. They walk the rest of the race that way, Derek leaning in on his father's shoulder, grimacing, walking on as his father holds him up. "I told him I was going to finish," Derek said later. "Then he said that we would do it together. So we did, and I limped over the line in tears."[100]

One day, we will arrive at the promised land of eternal rest. Some of us will sprint our last leg toward the finish with a final rush of adrenaline and effort. Others of us will seem to have barely made it, hobbling, weeping, hoping against hope. But whatever our condition, on that day we will have finished the race. We will see the one our hearts have longed for. And seeing him, we will be made be like him. There, we will know that from beginning to end, he has carried us.

Like a man carries his son, all the way until we came to that place of life and rest.

We are his beloved children, and "if we strive, he will help us. If we fail, he will cherish us. If we are guided by him, we shall overcome. If we overcome, we are sure to be crowned."[101] In this hope, we run, walk, fall, get up, muddle, and press on toward the finish—that on that day, he will present us blameless before his presence with great joy. To him be glory, majesty, dominion, and authority, before all time and now and forever. Amen.

AFTERWORD

ESTHER LIU

"I don't think I really struggle with this Christian perfectionism."

These were the first words I wrote in my journal after reading the initial chapters of this book. The thought stressed me out. On the one hand, I wondered how I would write an afterword for a book on a topic that I don't think I struggle with. But there was another stress. I wondered what was wrong with me—if I'm not a good enough Christian to even want to try to be perfect. After all, I am nowhere close to it. I have a mile-high list of specific things that I've done this past week that I know were unloving and unfaithful. I committed clear sins this morning. In addition, I am writing these very words two days after the deadline—a glaring reminder of my failures in time management.

Worst of all, despite pricks of remorse and guilt, I probably don't grieve over my sins as much as I should. These days, I find myself preoccupied with other desires and pursuits instead. My daily actions and decisions reveal that regardless of what I profess of my Christian faith, I've functionally been more anxious about getting what I want in life—some earthly version of love, safety, security, and comfort—than I've been anxious of whether my way of living is pleasing or displeasing to God.

"I'm not sure I'm trying to obey God as much as I'm just trying to avoid disobeying him too grievously," I continued to write in my journal. "My conscience must be too numbed or calloused to even really lament over my imperfections." How is this for an afterword?

Chances are, if you have reached the end of this book, you *do* resonate with the Christian perfectionism spoken of here. (After reading more chapters, I realize that I do too—I just needed help to see it.) But perhaps you don't, or perhaps there are people in your life who wouldn't, or perhaps you won't in a later season of life.

Yet wherever you find yourself, I hope that you were able to discover the beauty of your Savior once more through these pages. Whether you feel wholehearted desire to obey and love him today or not. Whether you're in a season of steady growth or feeling like your sins are more than the hairs on your head. Whether you care about your relationship with God and what he thinks, or are more apathetic than you'd like to admit. I hope that whether in desire or apathy, growth or stagnancy or backsliding, caring or not caring, you were able to behold your knowing, patient, loving God. He is the one who knows all of you and is committed to you in love. The one who sees your failings, pursues you in your waywardness, and invites you to himself—extending mercy to you as you receive his invitation. The one who delights to lead you, wants to see you succeed and flourish, and will carry you to the end. The reality is, the Savior held forth for us in this book is who we all need.

For myself? The words on these pages reminded me of spiritual aspirations that I once oriented my life around but that I unknowingly buried and gradually gave up on in discouragement. These pages renewed my vision to see the joy and blessing of living more fully for him. They made me remember the people in my life who taught me the heart of God through their own steady love towards me—one of those people being Faith Chang herself, a dear friend whose presence has forever changed me for the better since meeting her when I was 19 years old. The words on these pages also exposed specific moments of past and present sins that I had never brought to God—but I did a few days ago, with a grateful heart, knowing that the confession was received in his undeserved favor. These pages revealed fears that I didn't realize were gnawing at my heart—fears that I've made wrong decisions, that I have or will miss God's best, that perhaps I am the one sheep who won't hear his voice as clearly as I should, and that he may allow me to wander off to my own destruction and lostness. These pages revealed my ongoing wrestlings—whether I'll ever truly believe that God's love exceeds a mere tolerating of me, whether I can trust he will work out all things for good despite my blunders, if there really is hope for me in the innumerable ways in which I don't feel good enough today.

All this to say, I started this book as a very imperfect person, and I am finishing it still very imperfect. I am realizing this is and will be a journey... to know and believe the spiritual realities written here and to live as if they are true. That journey will be comprised of a thousand baby steps of growth, one step at a time. It will be marked by victories and failures, unlearning and relearning, joy and sorrow, moments of feeling encouraged and discouraged. But it's a journey that I want to finish, and finish well—because Christ is worthy.

I hope that through the pages of this book, we have all found deepened hope in our respective journeys that he is who he says he is, and he'll do what he says he'll do—in us, through us, and with us. I hope we've found even a small glimmer of comfort and assurance that we are so loved in it all. And in his goodness, I hope we have found some rest for our souls until we reach our eternal and perfect rest with him. *Soli Deo Gloria.* Glory to God alone.

Esther Liu
Counselor and Faculty Member,
Christian Counseling and Educational Foundation (CCEF)
Author, *Shame: Being Known and Loved*

DISCUSSION QUESTIONS AND FURTHER RESOURCES

The Christian perfectionist's journey toward rest is not meant to be taken alone. We need others to listen to us, pray for us, and gently remind us that God is more gracious, patient, and loving than we've dared to hope. We need others to muddle along with us in our pursuit of God and his rest.

These discussion questions are meant to facilitate some of that. You can use them as prompts for discussion as you read through this book with a trusted friend or in a small group. After sharing your answers, take time to pray for one another and the specific things that were shared. If you are reading alone, you can use these as journaling or reflection questions. For some chapters, I've included references you can use for further study.

INTRODUCTION

1. What brings you to this book?
2. How do you feel as you start it?
3. What are you hoping for in this study?

CHAPTER 1: THE PERFECTIONIST'S ACHE

1. How is the longing for perfection a reflection of fallenness in the world? Where do you tend to feel the world's brokenness most?
2. How does Christian perfectionism play out in your life? What has formed your "perfectionistic strivings"? When did you begin to feel "perfectionistic concerns"?
3. Read Matthew 11:28-30. What stands out to you about Jesus' words? How do you feel, knowing that Jesus invites the weary and heavy laden to come to him?

CHAPTER 2: KNOWLEDGE

1. Read Psalm 139. What is God's knowledge of us like? How does he think of us?
2. How have you tried to address your spiritual perfectionism in the past? What has helped? What hasn't?
3. What do you think are some possible roots of your own struggle with perfectionism? (It's ok if you're not sure.) How does it feel to know that God understands your burden?
4. Read John 10:1-18, 27-30. How does Jesus describe himself? How does he relate to his sheep? How does he relate to you?
5. What difference would it make for you to believe that you are fully known and fully loved?

Further study: *Shame: Being Known and Loved* by Esther Liu

CHAPTER 3: MERCY

1. Read Luke 18:9-14. Do you relate to the Pharisee or the tax collector? (Or both?) In what ways?
2. How does Jesus justify sinners? What difference does it make for you to remember that Christ was perfectly obedient for you?
3. Can you identify any recurrent accusations you face, which are not from God but Satan? How can you respond the next time they come up?
4. Look up the full text of John Newton's "These Inward Trials" and read it. Are there any parts of it that resonate with you? How have you seen God use inward trials in your life?

Further study: *A Bruised Reed* by Richard Sibbes

CHAPTER 4: LAW

1. Do you struggle with "doubts about [your] actions" in your walk with God? How and when?
2. Read Psalm 119:9-32. How does the psalmist describe God's law? How does he feel about it? How do you tend to approach God's commands?
3. How has this chapter prompted you to think differently about God's commands?
4. Are there any add-ons to God's law that you can identify in your life? Think about what you recurrently feel guilty about in your daily life. Where are your standards coming from? Are there any standards you're unsure about that you might need to re-examine in light of God's word?

Further study on distinguishing between God's law and...

- Tradition and personal convictions: *Conscience: What It Is, How to Train It, and Loving Those Who Differ* by Andrew David Naselli and J.D. Crowley
- Asceticism (regarding desire): *Teach Me to Want* by Jen Pollack Michel
- Finitude: *You're Only Human* by Kelly Kapic
- Stoicism (regarding emotions): *Untangling Emotions* by J. Alasdair Groves and Winston T. Smith
- Intrusive thoughts: *A Still and Quiet Mind* by Esther Smith
- Scrupulosity and OCD: "What is OCD and Scrupulosity?" from the International OCD foundation (https://iocdf.org/faith-ocd/what-is-ocd-scrupulosity/); Mike Emlet's article "Scrupulosity: When Doubts Devour" in the Journal of Biblical Counseling (https://www.ccef.org/shop/product/scrupulosity-when-doubts-devour-2/)

CHAPTER 5: PEACE

1. Read Luke 15. Are there any parts of the passage that stick out to you? How would you describe the shepherd, the woman, and the father? What do you notice about how God treats sinners in these parables?
2. How have you experienced God's welcome in your life?
3. When have you experienced the peace of knowing that things between you and God are good? When do you find that peace missing?
4. Are there ways in which you try to "justify your own existence"? How do you feel, knowing that you have no "use value" to God but that he simply loves you?

5. How can we help one another remember our belonging to Christ?

Further study: *The Prodigal God* by Timothy Keller

CHAPTER 6: PATIENCE

1. Do you struggle with the slowness of your sanctification? If so, in what areas? Does anything in this chapter shift your perspective on your sanctification?

2. Read Matthew 26:30-35, 69-75 and John 21:4-19. Does anything stick out to you in those passages? What is Jesus' attitude toward Peter and the disciples? How does it make you feel, knowing that this is how Jesus responds to your failures?

3. What difference has Jesus made in your life? How has he changed you since you've come to know him?

4. Sometimes, it's hard to see the way God is changing us. If you're using these questions with someone you know well, take time to affirm the ways you've seen God work in each other's lives. Alternatively, you could ask a trusted friend or spiritual mentor who has walked with you, "How have you seen God changing me?"

Further study: Skim through of one of the Gospels, writing down all the times when Jesus shows his patience. How does it make you feel, knowing that this is Jesus' posture toward you?

CHAPTER 7: PROVIDENCE

1. Read Psalm 127:1-2. What does it teach you about God? What does it teach you about yourself? What do you learn about God's providence?
2. Do you ever feel that life is a Rube Goldberg machine? When? What are the projections that you tend to make and consequences that you fear?
3. What difference would it make in your life for you to trust God's gracious providence in those situations? And his ability to use what is evil for good?
4. How have you seen God's grace over evil in your life? How might God be asking you to testify to this grace?

Further study: *Providence* by John Piper

CHAPTER 8: LOVE

1. When have you experienced God's love in your life?
2. When do you tend to say, "I know God loves me, but___"? How do you finish that sentence?
3. Read Galatians 2:20. Do you often think of Jesus' death on the cross as an act of love for you? If so, how has that impacted you? If not, what keeps you from seeing it as a demonstration of God's love for you?
4. Who is someone who has loved you well? What about their love touched or moved you? How was it a reflection of the love of God?
5. After reading this chapter, are there still any barriers to believing and receiving the love of God for you? Read Ephesians 3:14-17 and use it to guide yourself in prayer for yourself and one another.

Further study: *Gentle and Lowly* by Dane Ortlund

CHAPTER 9: THERE REMAINS A REST

1. Read Revelation 21:1-5 and 1 John 3:2-3. What is the future that is in store for us? What do you look forward to most about Jesus' return?

2. Where in your life have you been experiencing the "stretching of desire" in your longings for God's rest and perfection? How does Jesus' return shape the way you understand and respond to them?

3. Augustine prayed, "Grant what you command, and command what you wish." Have you experienced God working in you to do his will? When? Where do you need him to "grant what he commands" right now in your life?

4. Richard Sibbes writes, "If we strive, he will help us. If we fail, he will cherish us. If we are guided by him, we shall overcome. If we overcome, we are sure to be crowned." Do any of these "If... he..." statements encourage you? Which one and why?

5. As you come to the end of this study, how have you grown in your knowledge and experience of God? What has been most helpful to you? What would you like to explore more? What do you hope to carry from here as you continue to run your race?

Further study: *Even Better Than Eden* by Nancy Guthrie

ACKNOWLEDGMENTS

To the team at The Good Book Company, thank you for your love for God, his word, and people, which is so evident in all you do, including the choice to take a chance on this first-time author. Rachel J, thank you for believing in this book and for graciously and wisely making it so much better. Bethany M and Abigail T, thank you for your kindness, joy, and enthusiasm in helping get this book to readers.

To Esther L, it is a privilege to have your voice and words on these pages. Thank you for so beautifully demonstrating what it means to be a jar of clay.

To those who've given me courage in my writing journey, this book is a fruit of your generosity of spirit. WTS Bookstore team, thank you for your encouragement from the start. Friends at Reformed Margins and SOLA Network, thank you for helping me believe I have something worth sharing. Longtime blog readers, you have watered the seed of "maybe there's something more I could do here."

To friends who have prayed me through this project, read early versions, and cheered me on—Aaron L, Alfie A, Andrew C, Andrew O, Hanna N, Janice F, Josiah P, Kim L, Kyle W, Remley G, Sara W, Steph C, and Wednesday small-group ladies (Carol T, Lina H, Tammy Y)—thank you. God heard.

To brothers and sisters at GCC, I have learned to hope for our shared resurrection together with you. Thank you for helping me to remember and believe all the things I've written in this book, week in and week out.

To Mom and Dad Chang, Campbell, and Linda, your wholehearted support of me truly is a gift from God. Alicia, KK, and Natalie, may you always know your great worth in the Maker's sight.

To the sibs—Caleb and Victoria, thank you for seeing the best in me always; it means more to me than you know. RC, thank you for your ministry of Ubereats and that (gentle) bop on the head; God knew I needed you in my corner. A-girl, God answered your prayers for Auntie Faith's book! A, E, and M, may you always know the Father's delight and welcome many others home.

To Mom and Dad, thank you for showing me what it means to walk with God and be continually transformed by him into his image. My writing is a fruit of your prayers, guidance, giving, and sacrificial love for me. Mom, thank you for teaching me to fear God. Dad, thank you for showing me the delight of my heavenly Father.

To the Chang kid crew, thank you for asking about and praying for this book, for cheering when I finished my first draft, and for your patience with me. Thanks for never complaining when I had to write, and for cleaning up (H), preparing food (E), coming for snuggles (J), and sitting next to me drawing (A) while I wrote. I love you and pray you'd know the love and worth of Jesus all the days of your life.

To Jeff, thank you for picking up my slack, taking out the kids, and telling me, "Go write." This book is an answer to your prayers—not just for the words but for the person who wrote them. Every page is a witness to God's love to me through you. I love you.

God, for your unfathomable grace and marvelous love, for opening my eyes to see your worth, for giving me your Son and making beauty out of ashes, please receive this book as an offering of praise.

ENDNOTES

1 D.A. Carson, "Perfectionisms," *Themelios*, Volume 35, Issue 1 (2010), p 2.

2 Charles Haddon Spurgeon, "Return unto Thy Rest," *Metropolitan Tabernacle Pulpit*, Volume 47 (Sept. 7, 1879). https://www.spurgeon. org/resource-library/sermons/return-unto-thy-rest/#flipbook (accessed on Mar. 8, 2023).

3 Joechim Stoeber, *The Psychology of Perfectionism* (Taylor and Francis, 2018), p 3, Kindle.

4 Joachim Stoeber and Patrick Gaudreau, "The advantages of partialling perfectionistic strivings and perfectionistic concerns: Critical issues and recommendations," *Personality and Individual Differences*, Volume 104 (January 2017), p 379-386. https://doi.org/10.1016/j.paid.2016.08.039

5 Joachim Stoeber and F. S. Stoeber "Domains of perfectionism: Prevalence and relationships with perfectionism, gender, age, and satisfaction with life," *Personality and Individual Differences*, Volume 46, Issue 4. (Mar. 2009), p 530–535. https://doi.org/10.1016/j. paid.2008.12.006

6 D.A. Carson, "Perfectionisms" (as above).

7 Zack Eswine, *Spurgeon's Sorrows* (Christian Focus, 2014), p 19, Kindle.

8 The Westminster Confession of Faith describes Adam and Eve's disobedience in this way: "By this sin they fell from their original righteousness and communion with God, and so became dead in sin, and wholly defiled in all the parts and faculties of soul and body. They being the root of all mankind, the guilt of this sin was imputed; and the same death in sin, and corrupted nature, conveyed to all their posterity descending from them by ordinary generation." WCF 6.2, 3. https:// www.opc.org/wcf.html (accessed on Mar. 8, 2024).

9 The Greek word for this idea is *telos*, meaning "end" or "purpose." Related to *telos* is *teleios*, the word translated as "perfect" in the New Testament.

10 D.A. Carson, "Perfectionisms" (as above).

11 Herman Ridderbos, *The Coming of the Kingdom* (P&R Publishing, 1962), p 254-255.

12 John Mayer, "Daughters" (2004).

13 Mike Emlet, "Scrupulosity: When Doubts Devour" *The Journal of Biblical Counseling* Volume 33, Issue 3 (2019), p 17.

14 As above.

15 Timothy Keller and Kathy Keller, *The Meaning of Marriage* (Penguin

Books, 2011), p 95.

[16] J.I. Packer, *Knowing God* (Intervarsity Press, 1973 retypeset 2018), p 42.

[17] C.S. Lewis, *The Weight of Glory: And Other Addresses* (HarperCollins, 1980), p 38.

[18] J.I. Packer, *Knowing God* (as above), p 41.

[19] Mike Emlet talk about the tendency of perfectionists to focus on rules over relationship in his lecture "Perfectly Dreadful: Recognizing and Overcoming Perfectionism," given during the 2012 Christian Counseling & Educational Foundation National Conference.

[20] Ian Osborn, *Can Christianity Cure Obsessive-Compulsive Disorder?* (BrazosPress, 2008), p 19, Kindle.

[21] Richard Sibbes, *The Bruised Reed* (Banner of Truth, 2021), p 6.

[22] Some people misuse Scripture to take advantage of another person's desire to honor God in abusive ways. Darby Strickland has written a chapter on spiritual abuse in the context of marriage in *Is It Abuse? A Biblical Guide to Identifying Domestic Abuse and Helping Victims* (P&R Publishing, 2020). Much of her teaching on spiritual abuse can also be found from an online search. If you are a victim of domestic abuse and don't know where to find help, you can always call the National Domestic Violence Hotline at 800-799-SAFE (7233) in the US; or in the UK, the National Domestic Abuse Helpline on 0808 2000 247 or the Men's Advice Line on 0808 8010327.

[23] Horatius Bonar, *God's Way of Peace* (Christian Focus, 2021), p 17.

[24] *The Heidelberg Catechism*, English Translation (Faith Alive Christian Resources 2011). https://www.crcna.org/sites/default/files/HeidelbergCatechism.pdf (accessed on Aug. 12, 2022).

[25] Richard Sibbes, *The Bruised Reed* (as above), p 5.

[26] As above, p 12.

[27] As above, p 5.

[28] As above, p 71.

[29] C.S. Lewis, *Yours, Jack: Spiritual Direction from C.S. Lewis* (Harper One, 2008), p 312.

[30] An earlier version of the following story was shared in "God Who Waits" https://keepingheart.com/2019/03/14/god-who-waits/.

[31] Joachim Stöber, "The Frost Multidimensional Perfectionism Scale revisited: More perfect with four (instead of six) dimensions," *Personality and Individual Differences,* Volume 24, Issue 4 (April 1998), p 486. https://doi.org/10.1016/S0191-8869(97)00207-9

[32] Charles H. Spurgeon, *The Treasury of David: Psalms,* Volume 5

(Marshall Brothers, 1869), p 228, Logos Bible Software.

[33] John Calvin, *Institutes of the Christian Religion*, Book I:13:1.

[34] I first came across the idea of "calibrating" our consciences in this article by Andy Naselli: "Don't Always Follow Your Conscience," https://www. desiringgod.org/articles/dont-always-follow-your-conscience, (accessed on May 10, 2023).

[35] Cheryl Strayed, *Wild* (Oprah's Book Club 2.0 Digital Edition) (Knopf Doubleday Publishing Group, 2021) Kindle.

[36] Gordon L. Flett, Paul L. Hewitt, Taryn Nepon, and Avi Besser, "Perfectionism Cognition Theory," *The Psychology of Perfectionism*, ed. Joachim Stöber (Routledge/Taylor and Francis, 2018), p 102 Kindle.

[37] Jen Pollock Michel, *Teach Us to Want* (InterVarsity Press, 2014), p 23, Kindle.

[38] Mike Emlet, "Scrupulosity: When Doubts Devour," *The Journal of Biblical Counseling Volume* 33, Issue 3 (2019), p 12-13.

[39] Esther Smith, *A Still and Quiet Mind* (P&R Publishing, 2022), p 135.

[40] For example, freed from feeling like it's a sin to miss daily morning devotions, you find another way to practically obey the command to meditate on God's word day and night. Or, knowing there's more than one way to be involved in God's call to make disciples of all nations, you ask God, "What's my part in global missions?," discerning and obeying his leading in community. For further help regarding some of the specific "add-ons" I've listed, I've included resources for further study in the appendix.

[41] See the appendix for resources for further understanding the issue of "scrupulosity" or "religious OCD."

[42] Cheryl Strayed, *Wild* (as above), p 107, Kindle.

[43] Kelly Kapic, *You're Only Human* (Brazos Press: 2022), p 23.

[44] As above, p 24.

[45] As above.

[46] Horatius Bonar, *God's Way of Peace* (Christian Focus, 2021), p 137.

[47] Frequent and prolonged rumination is another feature of perfectionism. Perfectionists tend to have an "overdeveloped memory for mistakes, failures, and stressful experiences that highlight a sense of personal inadequacy." Gordon L. Flett, Paul L. Hewitt, Taryn Nepon, and Avi Besser, "Perfectionism Cognition Theory," (as above) p 99, Kindle.

[48] Ed Welch, "Holiness Is Not Our Goal", https://www.ccef.org/holiness-not-goal/, (accessed on Nov. 29, 2022).

[49] Mike Emlet, "Religious OCD", Lecture from 2011 Christian

Counseling & Educational Foundation National Conference.

[50] I first came across this idea of working from peace versus for peace in Matt Perman's *What's Best Next* (Zondervan, 2014), p 120.

[51] Walter L. Liefeld, "Luke" in *The Expositor's Bible Commentary: Matthew, Mark, Luke* (Vol. 8), ed. Frank E. Gaebelein (Zondervan Publishing House, 1984), p 985.

[52] *The Heidelberg Catechism*, (as above), https://www.crcna.org/welcome/beliefs/confessions/heidelberg-catechism (accessed on Nov 29, 2022).

[53] Alan Noble, "On Living," https://thealannoble.medium.com/on-living-3363ce5bb6ac (accessed on Nov. 29, 2022).

[54] J. Gresham Machen, *Things Unseen* (Westminster Seminary Press, 2020), p 76.

[55] Mary Oliver, "Don't Worry," *Felicity* (Penguin Books, 2017), p 3.

[56] Benjamin B. Warfield, *The Works of Benjamin B. Warfield: Perfectionism, Part Two,* Volume 8 (Logos Bible Software, 2008), p 561.

[57] B.B. Warfield points this out in *The Works of Benjamin B. Warfield: Perfectionism, Part One,* Volume 7 (Logos Bible Software, 2008), p 117–118.

[58] Martin Luther "The Ninety-Five Theses," https://tabletalkmagazine.com/article/2017/10/ninety-five-theses/ (accessed on Mar. 8, 2023).

[59] I don't recall where I first heard about how this miracle relates to God's usual work of sanctification in our lives.

[60] D. Martyn Lloyd-Jones, "Where Is Your Faith?" https://www.mljtrust.org/sermons-online/luke-8-22-25/where-is-your-faith/ (accessed on Nov. 29, 2022).

[61] John Newton, *One Hundred and Twenty Nine Letters from the Rev. John Newton Late Rector of St. Mary Woolnoth, London to the Rev. William Bull, of Newport Pagnell: Written During a Period of Thirty-two Years, from 1773 to 1805* (Hamilton, Adams, & Company, 1847) p 262, Google Books.

[62] David Brooks, "Suffering Fools Gladly," *The New York Times*, https://www.nytimes.com/2013/01/04/opinion/brooks-suffering-fools-gladly.html (accessed on Nov. 29, 2022).

[63] Quoted by Arthur W. Pink, *The Nature of God* (Moody Publishers, 1999), p 74.

[64] As above.

[65] Sarah J. Egan and Roz Shafran, "Cognitive-Behavioral Treatment for Perfectionism," in *The Psychology of Perfectionism*, (as above), p 295 Kindle.

[66] Sibbes points this out in *The Bruised Reed* (as above), p 24.

[67] Kevin Deyoung, *The Hole in Our Holiness* (Crossway, 2014), p 138.

[68] As above.

[69] If you are feeling hopeless, whether because of spiritual discouragement or something else, please reach out to a trusted friend or leader, doctor, or mental-health professional. If you don't have someone to talk to, you can call or chat online with someone at the National Suicide & Crisis Lifeline anytime at https://988lifeline.org (in the US) or call Samaritans on 116 123 (in the UK). There is nothing un-Christian about needing help. You are loved, worthy, and needed here.

[70] John Piper, "Why God Is Not a Megalomaniac in Demanding to Be Worshiped," Evangelical Theological Society (ETS) Annual Meeting on Nov. 20, 2008, https://www.desiringgod.org/messages/why-god-is-not-a-megalomaniac-in-demanding-to-be-worshiped (accessed on Nov. 29, 2022).

[71] Mary Oliver, "Don't Worry," *Felicity* (as above), p 3.

[72] Jonathan Rogers, "Cunning and Prudence: Some Thoughts on Persuasion," https://rabbitroom.com/2020/11/cunning-and-prudence-some-thoughts-on-persuasion/ (accessed on May 10, 2023).

[73] Perfectionists tend to imagine the worst possible outcome of their mistakes (also known as "catastrophic beliefs") and often have an overdeveloped sense of personal responsibility. Gordon L. Flett, Paul L. Hewitt, Taryn Nepon, and Avi Besser, "Perfectionism Cognition Theory," (as above), p 98, Kindle.

[74] Some might also use the term "sovereignty" interchangeably with how I'll be using "providence" in this chapter.

[75] *The Heidelberg Catechism* (as above) (accessed on Feb. 25, 2023).

[76] Elisabeth Elliot, *Passion and Purity* (Revell, 2021), p 45-46, Kindle.

[77] J.I. Packer, *Knowing God* (as above), p 241.

[78] I've written about this in an article for SOLA Network entitled "Combating Perfectionism in Communal Culture," https://sola.network/article/combating-perfectionism-in-communal-culture/ (accessed on Feb. 25, 2023). Also see J. Yoon and A. S. Lau, "Maladaptive perfectionism and depressive symptoms among Asian American college students: Contributions of interdependence and parental relations," *Cultural Diversity and Ethnic Minority Psychology*, Volume 14, Issue 2, (2008), p 92–101. https://doi.org/10.1037/1099-9809.14.2.92 (accessed on Feb. 25, 2023).

[79] Christian Reformed Church, Service for Word and Sacrament (1981),

https://www.crcna.org/resources/church-resources/liturgical-forms/lords-supper/service-word-and-sacrament-1981 (accessed on Feb. 25, 2023).

[80] As above.

[81] Sinclair Ferguson, "God Meant It for Good" https://media-cloud.sermonaudio.com/text/629141710441.pdf (accessed on Mar. 13, 2023).

[82] James K.A. Smith, *How to Inhabit Time* (Baker Publishing, 2023), p 61.

[83] As above, p 61-62.

[84] John Newton, "That bitter root, indwelling sin!" https://www.gracegems.org/Newton/44.htm (accessed on May 10, 2023).

[85] Erik Raymond, "Basking in God's Love," https://www.placefortruth.org/blog/basking-in-gods-love (accessed on Feb. 27, 2023).

[86] Geerhardus J. Vos and Richard B. Gaffin (translator), *Reformed Dogmatics (Single Volume Edition): A System of Christian Theology* (Lexham Press, 2020), p 142.

[87] Kevin DeYoung, *The Hole in Our Holiness* (as above), p 69-70.

[88] Richard Sibbes, *The Bruised Reed* (as above), p 7.

[89] George Herbert, "Love (III)," https://www.poetryfoundation.org/poems/44367/love-iii (accessed on Feb. 27, 2023).

[90] Jonny Robinson, Nigel Hendroff, Rich Thompson, "It Was Finished upon That Cross," 2021 CityAlight Music.

[91] Geerhadaus Vos, *Biblical Theology: Old and New Testaments* (Wipf & Stock Publishers, 2003), p 140.

[92] Augustine of Hippo, "Ten Homilies on the First Epistle of John," in P. Schaff (ed.), H. Browne and J.H. Myers (trans.), *St. Augustin: Homilies on the Gospel of John, Homilies on the First Epistle of John, Soliloquies* Volume 7 (Christian Literature Company, 1888, p 484-485.

[93] Nancy Guthrie, *Even Better Than Eden* (Crossway, 2018), p 12.

[94] C.S. Lewis, The Space Trilogy, Omnibus Edition (HarperCollins, 2013), p. 422.

[95] The promise of eternal life was hinted at in Genesis by the presence of (and after the fall, prohibition regarding) the tree of life in Eden. It is revealed more clearly in the New Testament, where Jesus is described as humanity's "second Adam," whose obedience merited eternal life where the first Adam had failed (Romans 5:12-21; 1 Corinthians 15:22). For an accessible explanation of this, see Nancy Guthrie's *Even Better Than Eden* (Crossway, 2018). See also this article from Ligonier ministries on covenants in Reformed theology: https://www.ligonier.org/learn/series/what-is-reformed-theology/covenant (accessed on Mar. 29, 2023) and Justin Taylor's article "Why I Believe in the Covenant of Works":

https://www.thegospelcoalition.org/blogs/justin-taylor/why-i-believe-in-the-covenant-of-works/ (accessed on Mar. 29, 2023).

[96] C.S. Lewis, The Space Trilogy, Omnibus Edition (as above), p 435. Kindle.

[97] Newton writes, "The life of grace is the dawn of immortality, beautiful beyond expression, if compared with the night and thick darkness which formerly covered us; yet faint, indistinct, and unsatisfying, in comparison of the glory which shall be revealed." John Newton, "On the gradual increase of gospel illumination," https://www.gracegems.org/Newton/24.htm (accessed on Feb. 27, 2023).

[98] John Newton, "On the gradual increase of gospel illumination" (as above).

[99] Augustine, *Confesssions*, trans. Sarah Ruden (The Modern Library, 2018), p 314.

[100] Laurel Wamsley, "The father who helped his son cross the finish line at the Olympics has died," NPR, Oct. 4, 2022, https://www.npr.org/2022/10/04/1126776697/jim-redmond-derek-olympics-sprinter-father-dies (accessed on Feb. 18, 2022).

[101] Richard Sibbes, *The Bruised Reed* (as above), p 140.